RECORDED VERSIONS GUITAR

AUTHENTIC TRANSCRIPTIONS
WITH NOTES AND TABLATURE

B E N   H A R P E R   BOTH SIDES OF THE GUN

T0087799

Front cover photo by Michael Halsband
Music transcriptions by Jeff Jacobson and Paul Pappas

ISBN 1-4234-1219-2

HAL•LEONARD® CORPORATION
7777 W. BLUEMOUND RD. P.O. BOX 13819 MILWAUKEE, WI 53213

In Australia Contact:
Hal Leonard Australia Pty. Ltd.
4 Lentara Court
Cheltenham, Victoria, 3192 Australia
Email: ausadmin@halleonard.com

Visit Hal Leonard Online at
www.halleonard.com

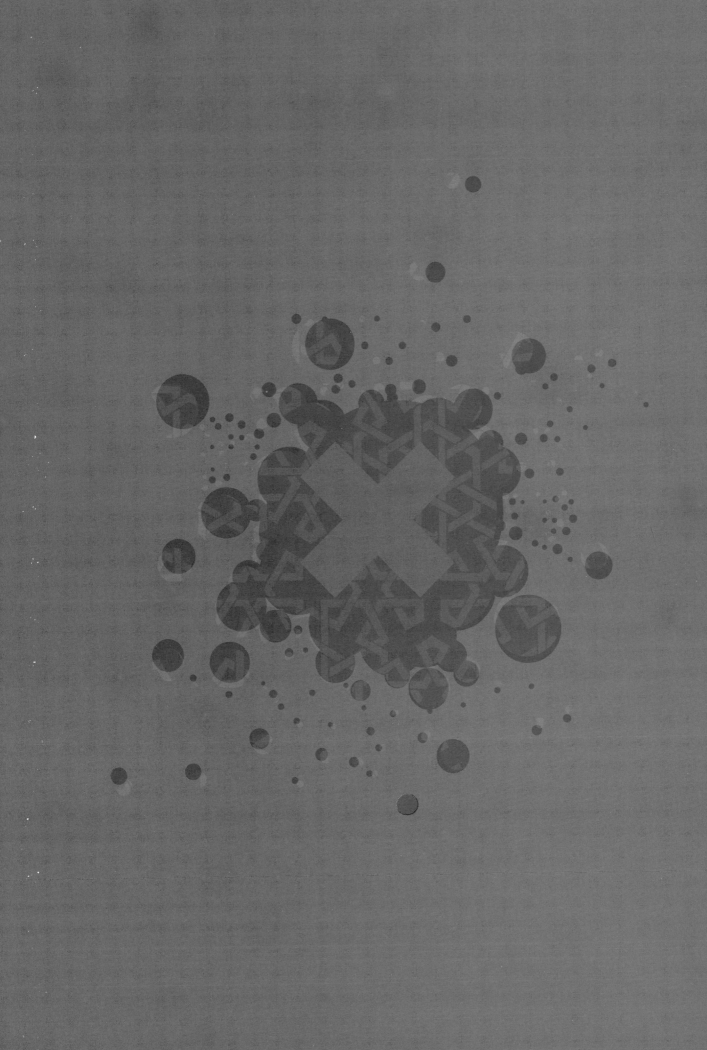

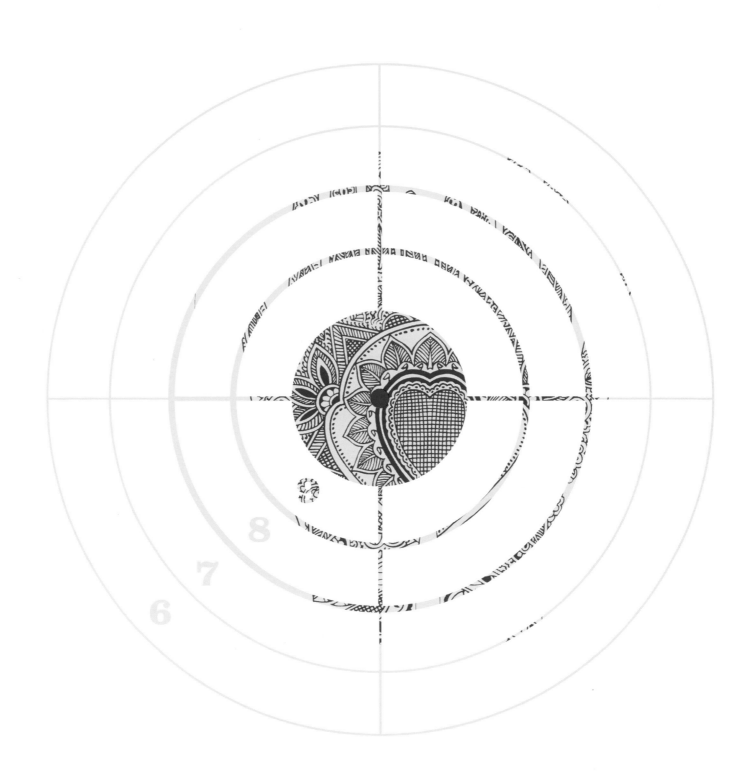

Morning Yearning

Words and Music by Ben Harper

Gtr. 1: Drop D tuning:
(low to high) D-A-D-G-B-E

Intro
Moderately slow ♩ = 76

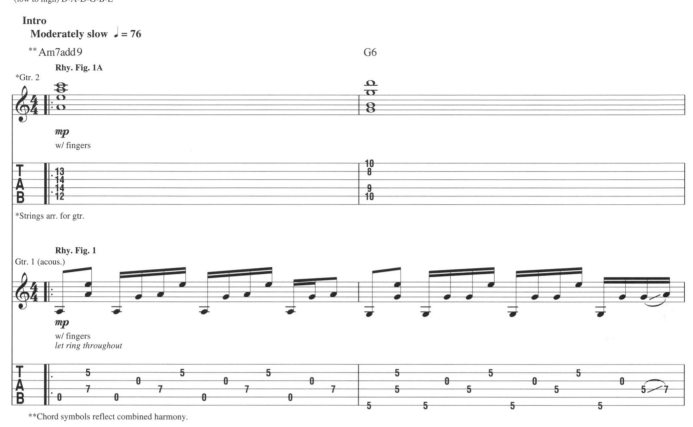

*Strings arr. for gtr.

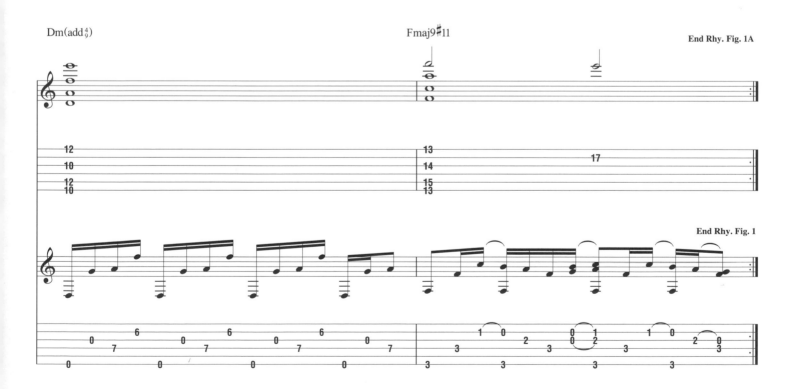

**Chord symbols reflect combined harmony.

Verse

Gtr. 1: w/ Rhy. Fig. 1 (3 times)
Gtr. 2 tacet

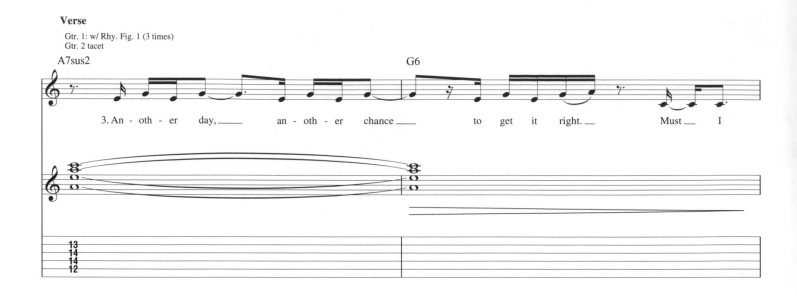

3. An - oth - er day,____ an - oth - er chance ____ to get it right.____ Must ____ I

Gtr. 3 tacet

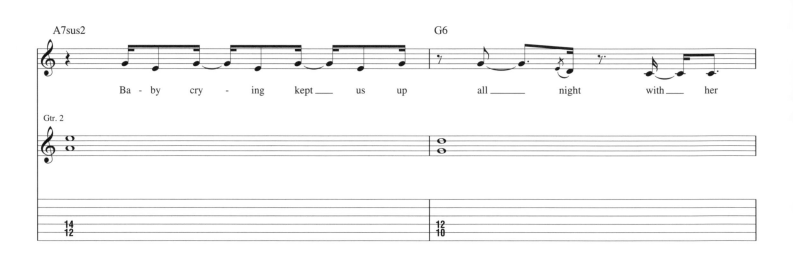

still be learn - ing?____ Must I still be learn - ing?_____

Baby cry - ing kept ____ us up all _____ night with ____ her

Gtr. 2

morn - ing _____ yearn - ing, ____ with her morn - ing yearn -

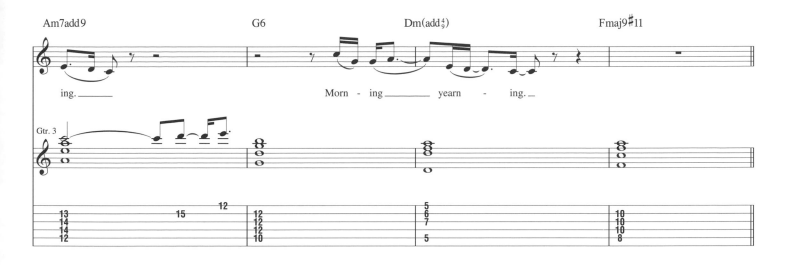

ing. _____   Morn - ing _____ yearn - ing.

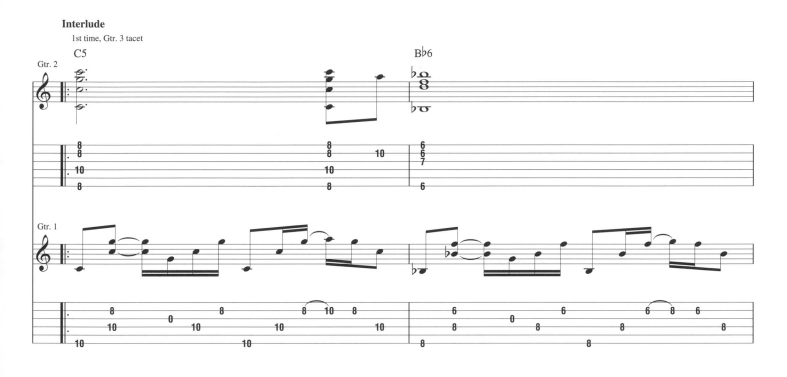

Interlude

1st time, Gtr. 3 tacet

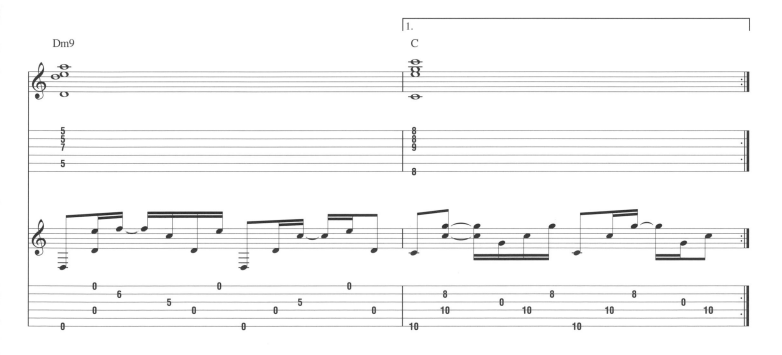

D.C. al Coda
(no repeats)

Coda

Gtr. 2: w/ Rhy. Fig. 1A
Gtr. 3: w/ Rhy. Fig. 2

Am7add9   G6   Dm(add4/9)   Fmaj9#11

Morn-ing _____ yearn - ing.

Am

Gtrs. 2 & 3
rit.

Gtr. 1
rit.

Waiting for You

Words and Music by Ben Harper and Michael Ward

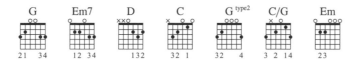

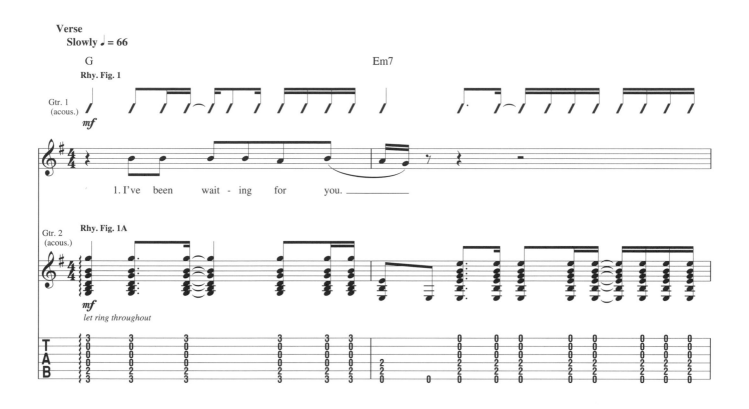

1. I've been wait - ing for you. ____

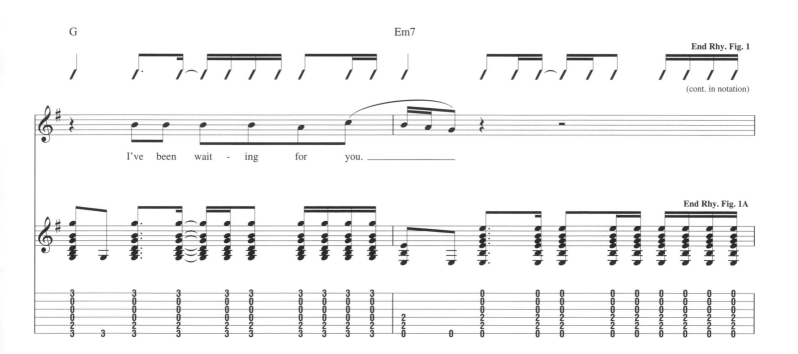

I've been wait - ing for you. ____

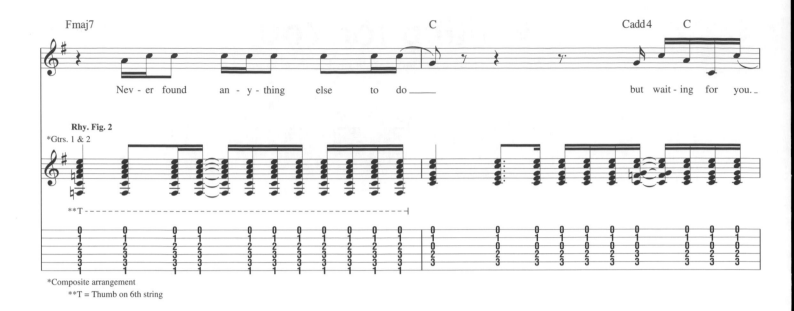

*Composite arrangement
  **T = Thumb on 6th string

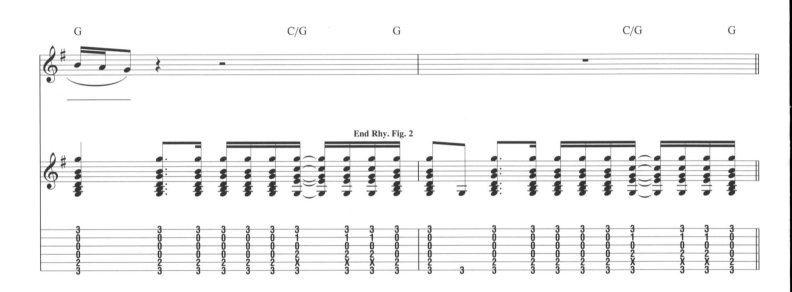

***Gtr. 3 (elec.) w/ clean tone, played *mf*. Composite arrangement
†Kybd. arr. for gtr.

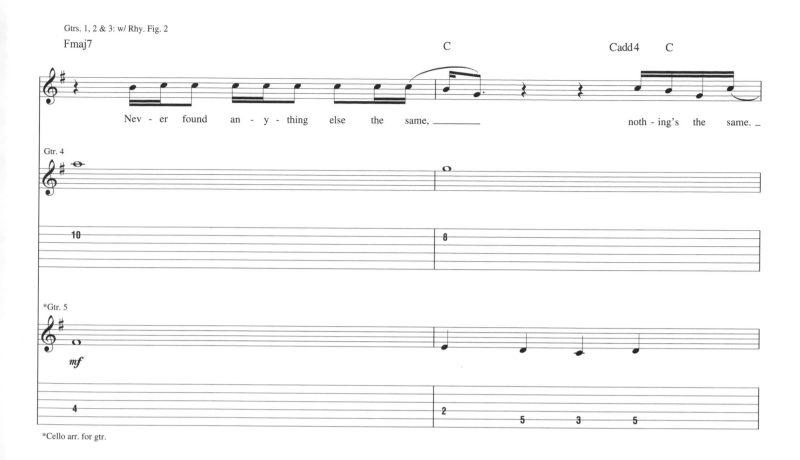

*Cello arr. for gtr.

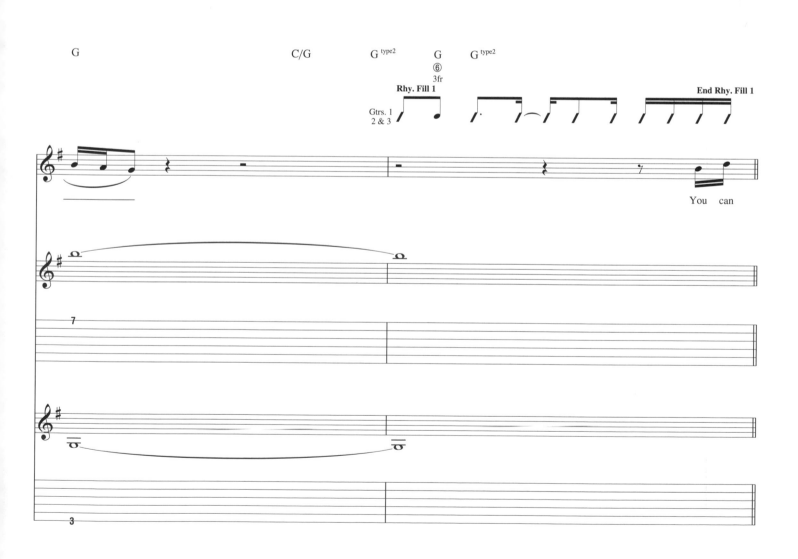

Verse

Gtr. 1: w/ Rhy. Fig. 1
Gtrs. 2 & 3: w/ Rhy. Fig. 1A
Gtr. 4 tacet

3. I keep hear-ing your name. ___   I keep hear-ing your name. ___

Gtrs. 1, 2 & 3: w/ Rhy. Fig. 2   Gtrs. 1, 2 & 3: w/ Rhy. Fill 1

Noth-ing else sounds the same ___   as hear-ing your name. ___   You can

Chorus

Gtrs. 1, 2 & 3: w/ Rhy. Fig. 3
Gtr. 4: w/ Rhy. Fig. 3A
Gtr. 5: w/ Riff A

kill a lot of time ___ if you real - ly put your mind to it, _____ or

leave it all be - hind ___ and nev - er ev - er go through it. _____

Interlude

Gtr. 1: w/ Rhy. Fig. 1
Gtrs. 2 & 3: w/ Rhy. Fig. 1A
Gtrs. 4 & 5 tacet

Chorus
Gtrs. 1, 2 & 3: w/ Rhy. Fig. 3 (2 times)
Gtr. 4: w/ Rhy. Fig. 3A (2 times)

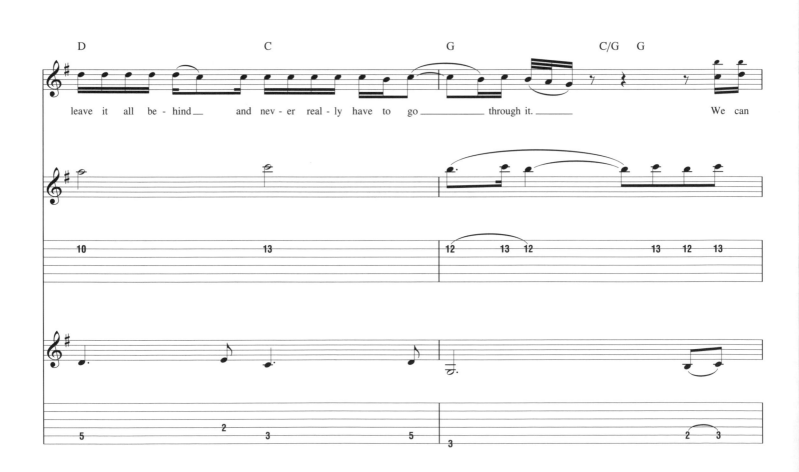

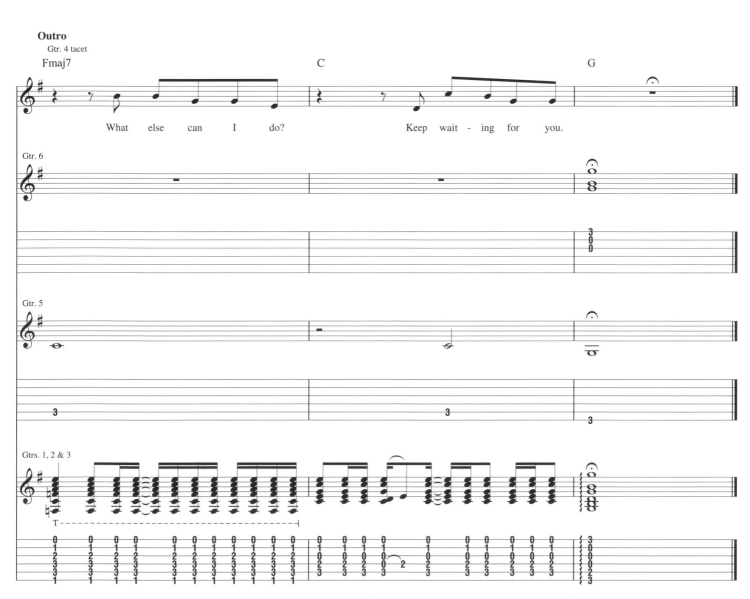

Picture Me in a Frame

Words and Music by Ben Harper, Michael Ward, Juan Nelson, Oliver Charles, Leon Mobley and Jason Yates

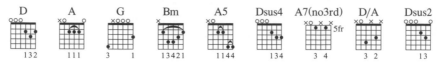

Drop D tuning:
(low to high) D-A-D-G-B-E

Intro

Moderately slow ♩ = 63

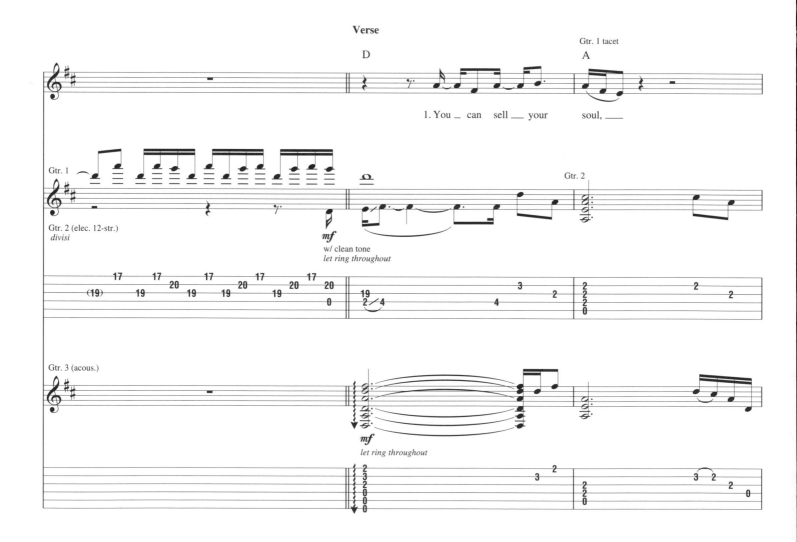

*Elec. piano arr. for gtr.

**Chord symbols reflect basic harmony.

but you can't___ buy it back.___ I've spent my___ whole life___

work - ing to give___ you ev - 'ry-thing___ you lack.___ I

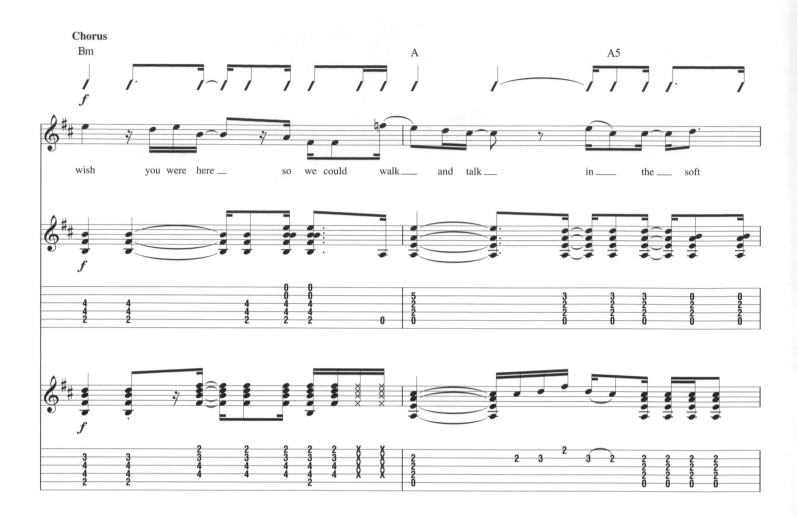

wish you were here ___ so we could walk ___ and talk ___ in ___ the ___ soft

rain, ___ in the ___ soft rain.

Now,_ all __ that's left __ of us   is a pic - ture   sit - ting   in a frame.__

to - mor - row.

Gtr. 5 (elec.)

f
w/ dist.
w/ slide

Gtr. 2

Gtr. 3

Chorus

wish   you __ were   here __   so   we could walk____   and   talk __   in __   the   soft __

no

no

Chorus

Bm   A

wish   you __ were here __   so we could walk____   and talk __   in __ the soft __

no

rain, _____ in the soft rain. _____ Now, all _____ that's left ___ of us ___ is a pic -

ture   sit - ting ___ in a frame, ___   a pic - ture in a frame. ___

(cont. in notation)

Bridge

Ev - 'ry - thing__ I wish for is ev - 'ry - thing__ I see. I re - mem - ber when your

35

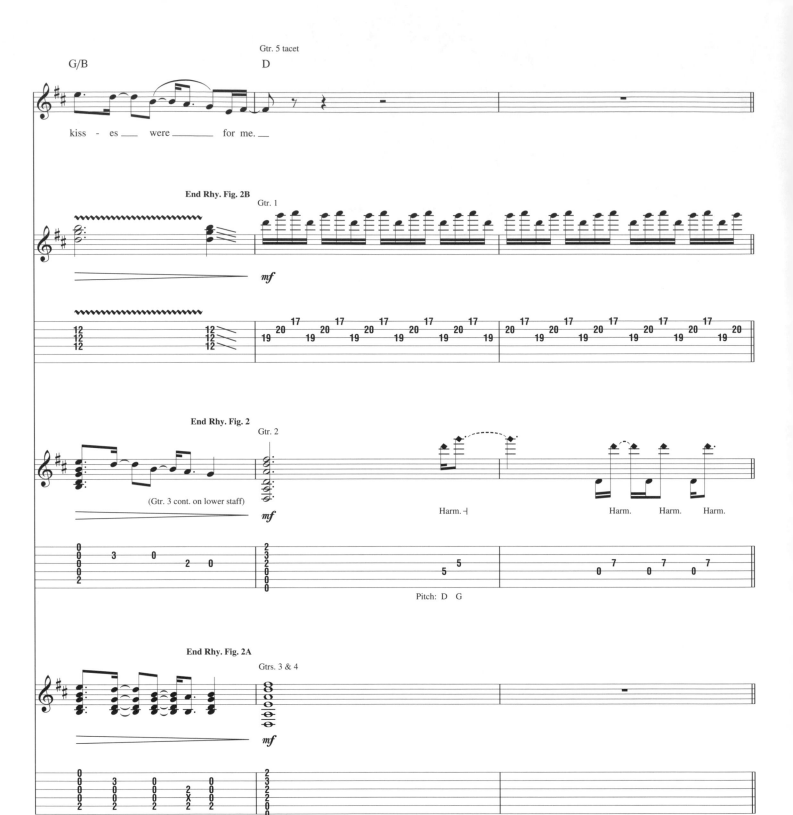

kiss - es ___ were ___ for me. ___

Verse

3. So man - y wast-ed days,_ the past is so __ hard to get out from un-

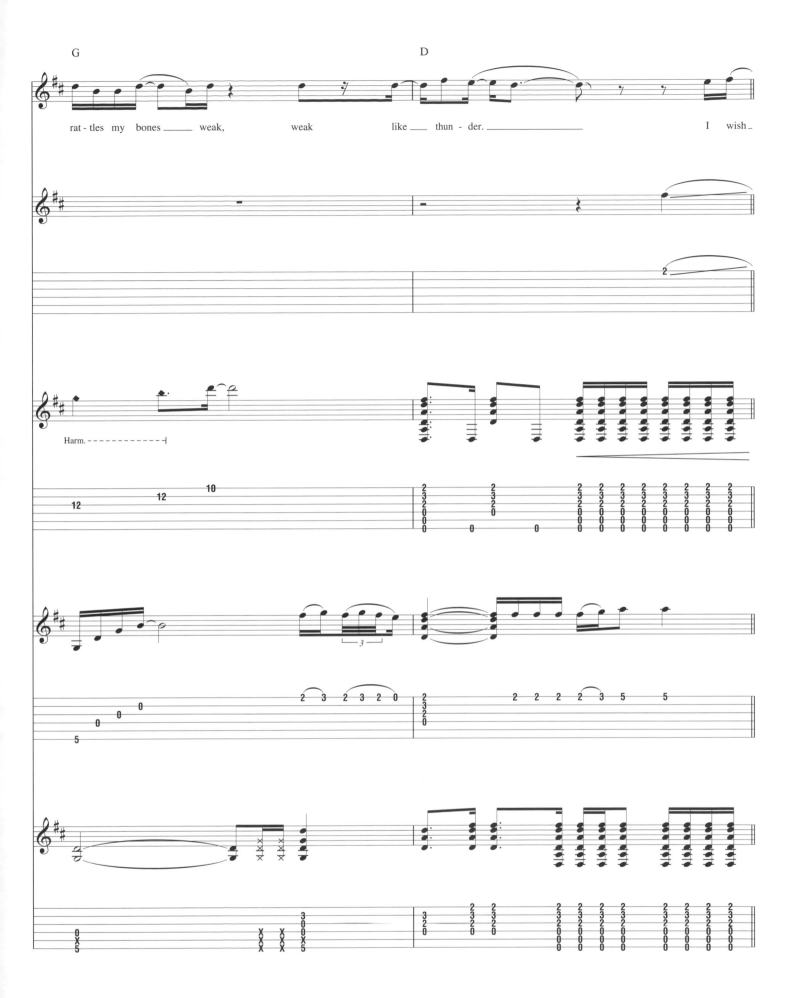

rat - tles my bones ____ weak,   weak   like ____ thun - der. _____   I wish _

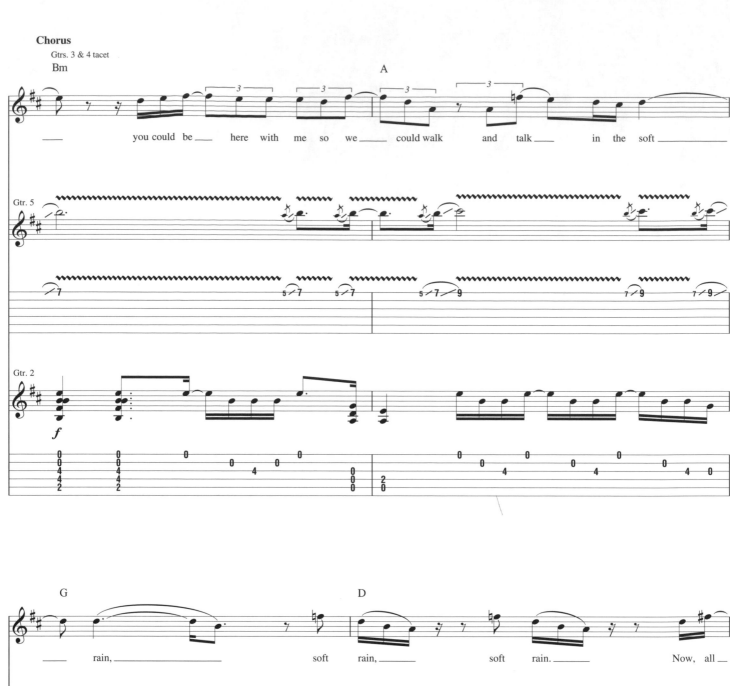

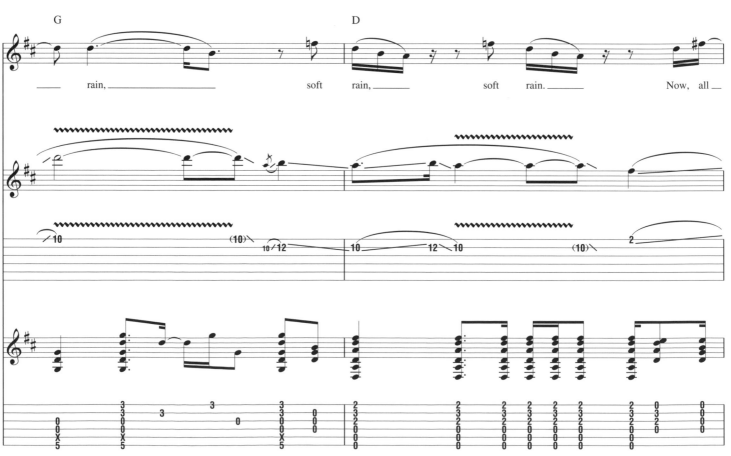

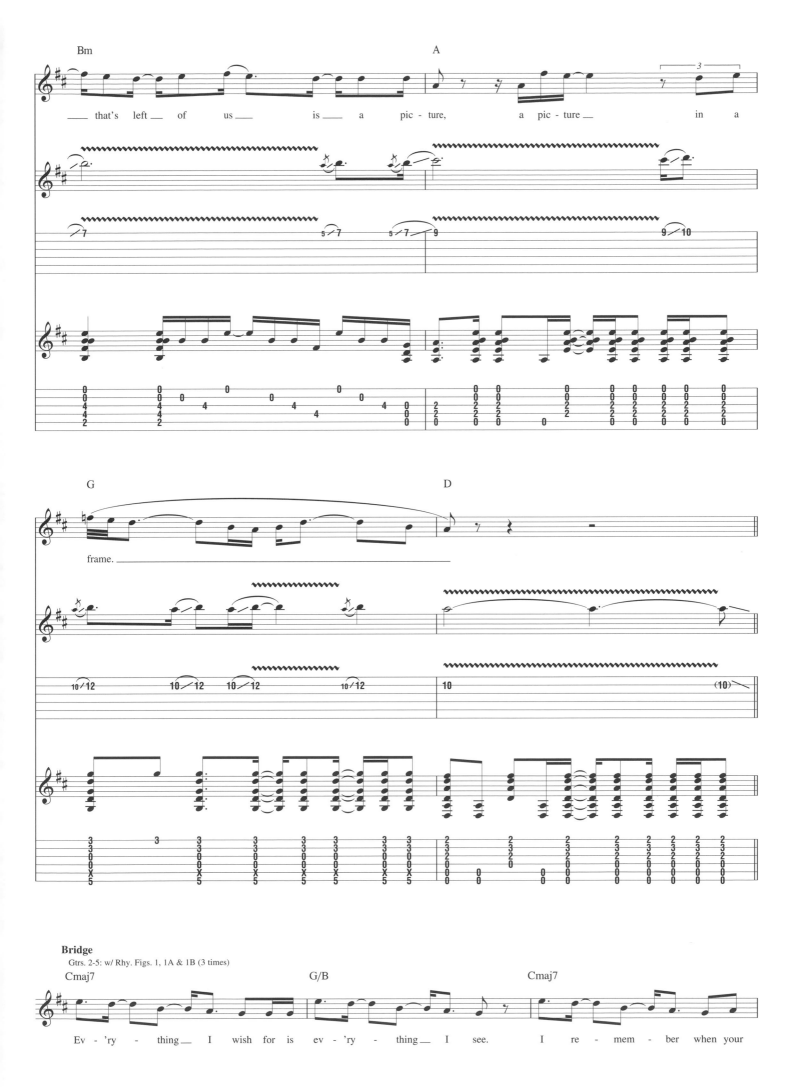

G/B   Cmaj7   G/B

kiss - es___ were___ for___ me.___   Ev-'ry-thing I wish___ for   is ev-'ry-thing I see.   I re-mem-

Gtrs. 2-5: w/ Rhy. Figs. 2, 2A & 2B

Cmaj7   G/B

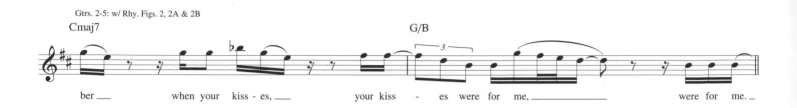

ber ___   when your kiss - es, ___   your kiss - es were for me, _____   were for me. _

Outro

Gtr. 5 tacet

*sol ponticello (pick near bridge w/ finger tip)

Never Leave Lonely Alone

Words and Music by Ben Harper

close your eyes __ does the world __ dis - ap - pear? _____

Coda

Outro

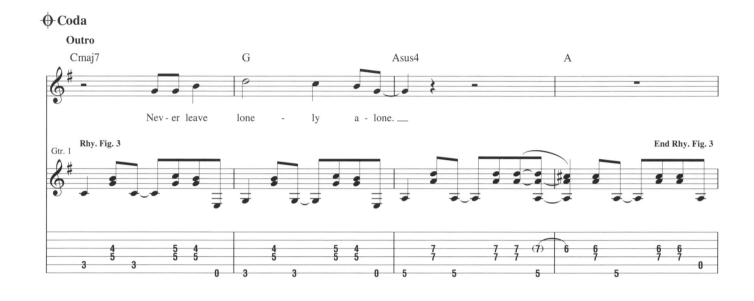

Nev - er leave lone - ly a - lone. __

Rhy. Fig. 3
Gtr. 1

End Rhy. Fig. 3

Gtr. 1: w/ Rhy. Fig. 3

Nev - er leave lone - ly a - lone. __

Nev - er leave lone - ly _____ a - lone. __

Sweet Nothing Serenade

(Instrumental)

By Ben Harper

Open E tuning, down 1 step:
(low to high) D-A-D-F♯-A D

Moderately ♩ = 100

*Gtr. 1 (acous.) (Drums)

**E

mf
w/ slide
w/ fingers

*Weissenborn Hawaiian gtr.   **Chord symbols reflect overall harmony.

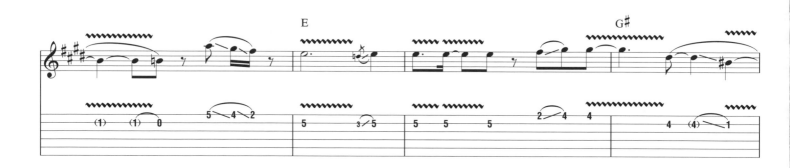

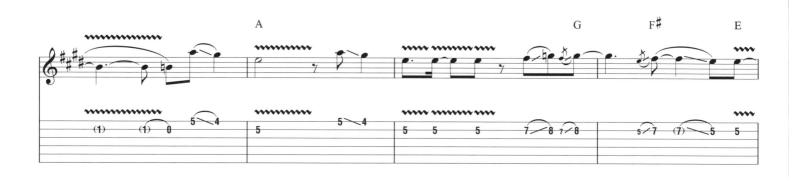

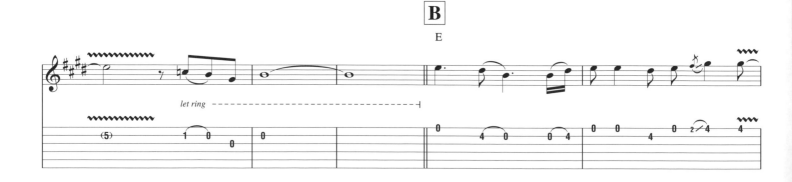

let ring

Reason to Mourn

Words and Music by Ben Harper

*Harmony is processed female vocal.

𝄋 Chorus

3rd time, Gtr. 2: w/ Fill 2

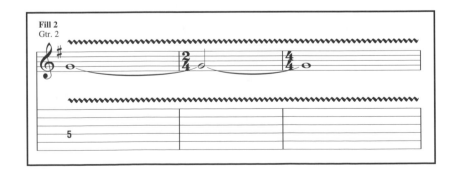

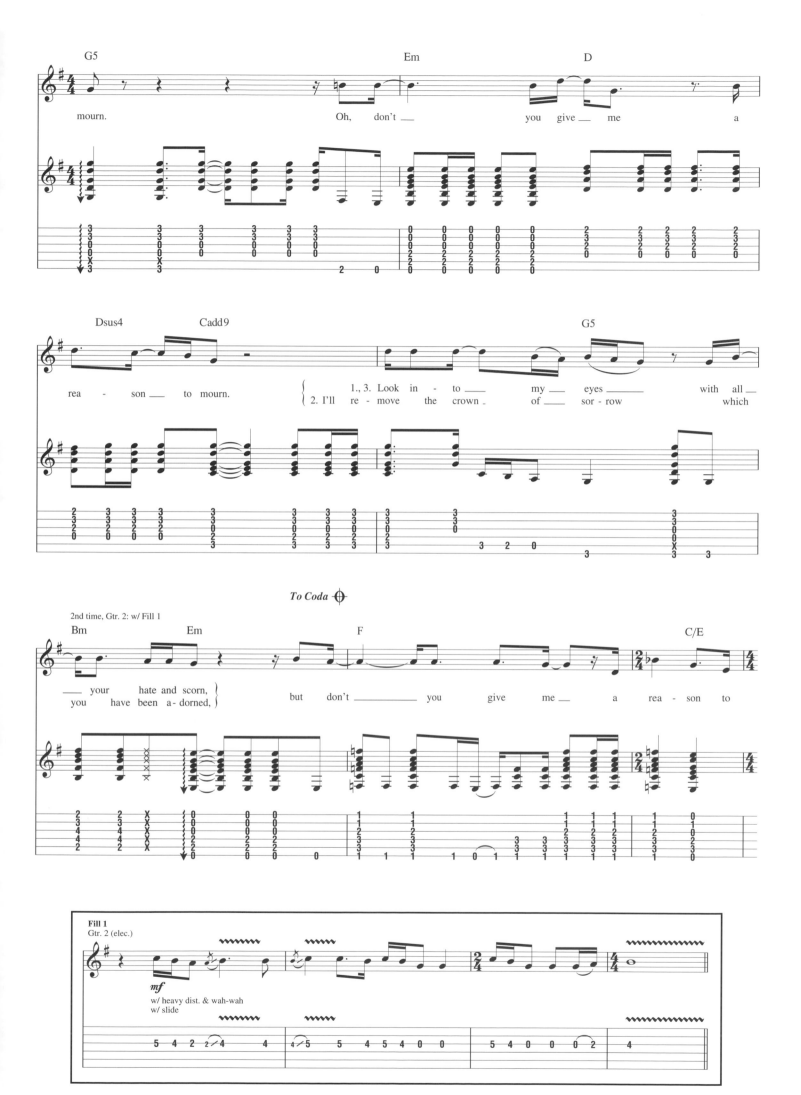

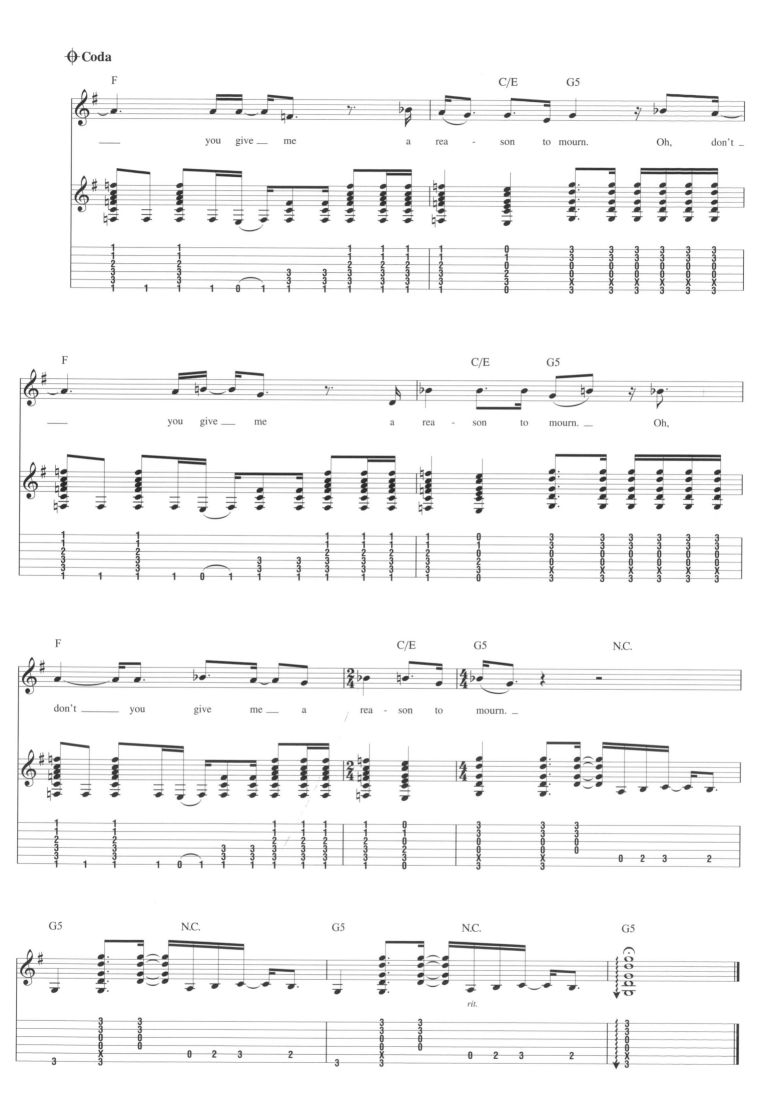

More Than Sorry

Words and Music by Ben Harper and Danny Kalb

Tune down 1 step:
(low to high) D-G-C-F-A-D

Intro
Moderately slow ♩ = 66

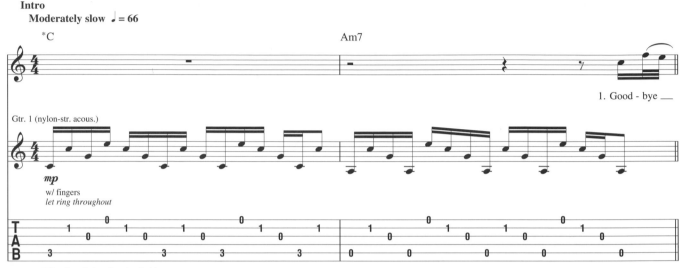

*Chord symbols reflect implied harmony.

Verse

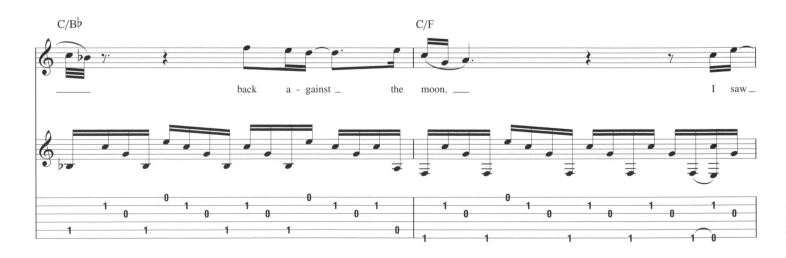

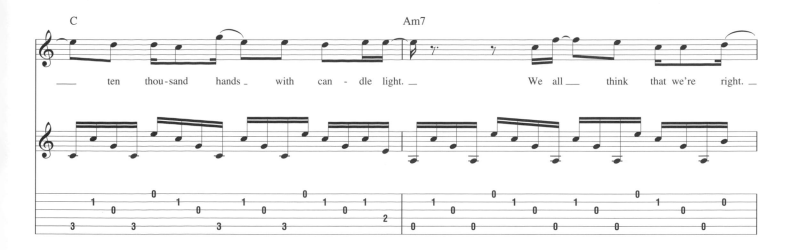

____ ten thou-sand hands ___ with can - dle light. ___ We all ___ think that we're right. ___

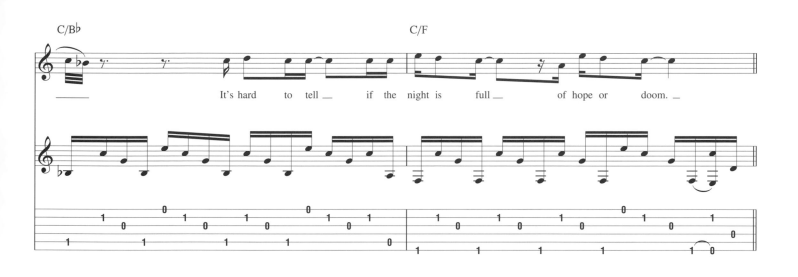

____ ___ It's hard to tell ___ if the night is full ___ of hope or doom. ___

Chorus

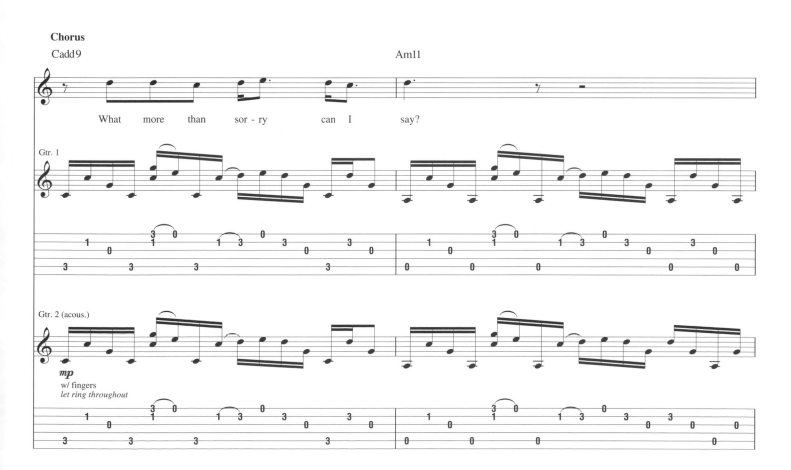

What more than sor - ry can I say?

Gtr. 1

Gtr. 2 (acous.)

mp
w/ fingers
let ring throughout

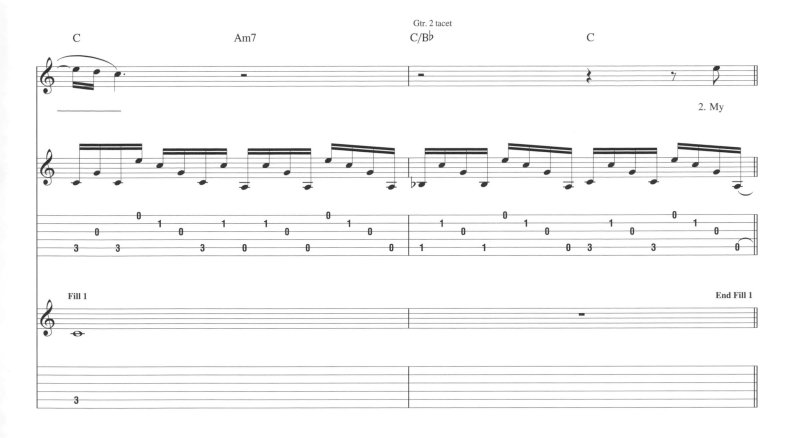

Gtr. 2 tacet

C   Am7   C/B♭   C

2. My

Fill 1   End Fill 1

Verse

Cadd9   Am11

eyes ____   burn with un - shed tears. ___   My bod - y is weak ___

Gtr. 1

C6/B♭   C6/F

____   from so man - y si - lent years.

Too man-y peo-ple say good-bye be-fore they say____ hel-lo,

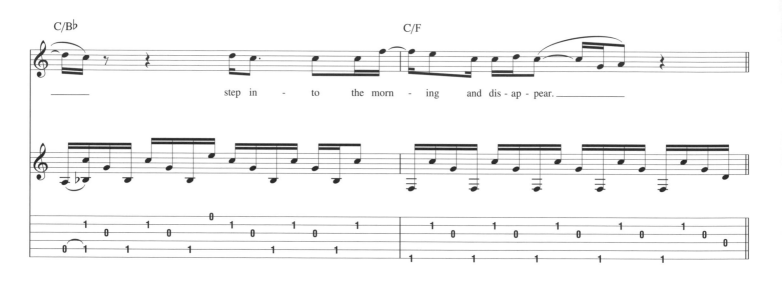

____ step in - to the morn - ing and dis-ap-pear.____

Chorus

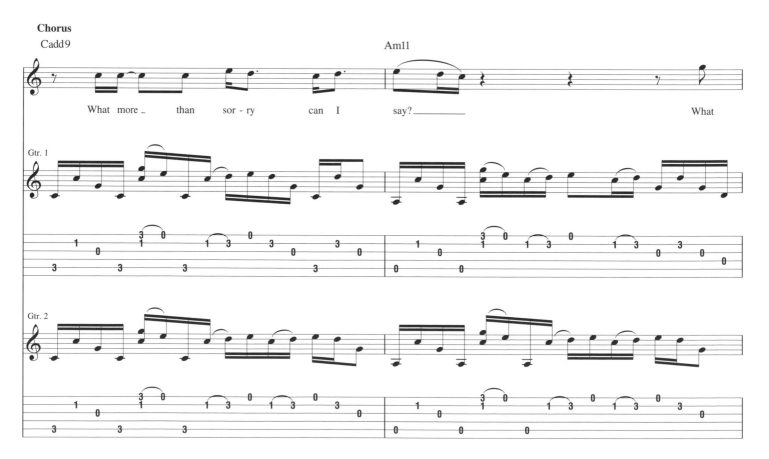

What more _ than sor - ry can I say?____ What

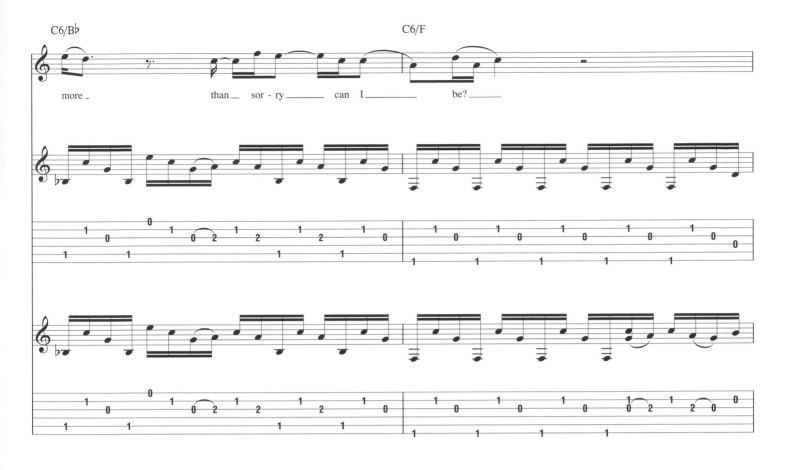

more _____ than _____ sor - ry _____ can I _____ be? _____

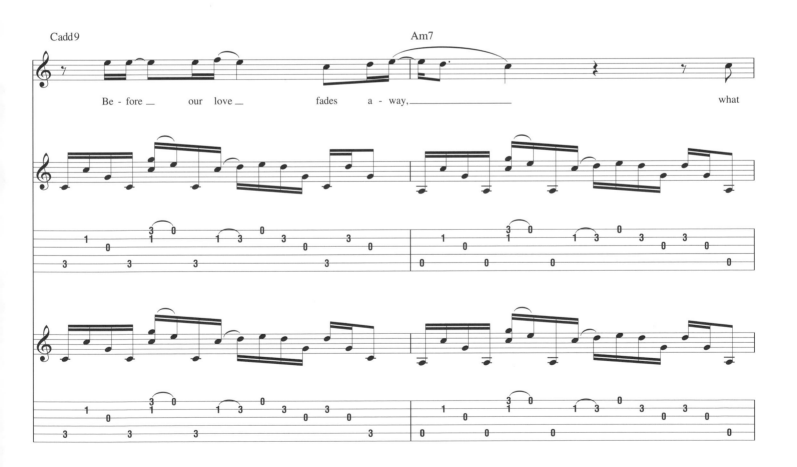

Be - fore _____ our love _____ fades a - way, _____ what

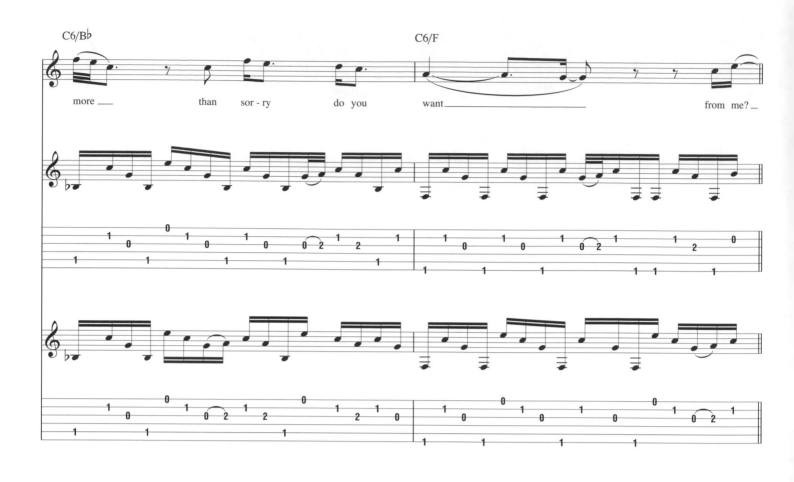

more ___ than sor-ry do you want ___ from me? __

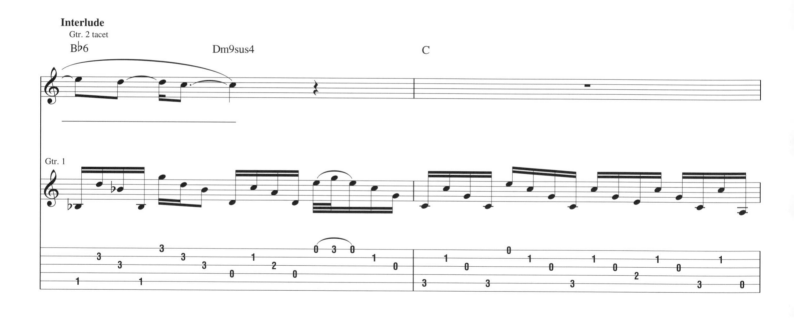

Interlude
Gtr. 2 tacet

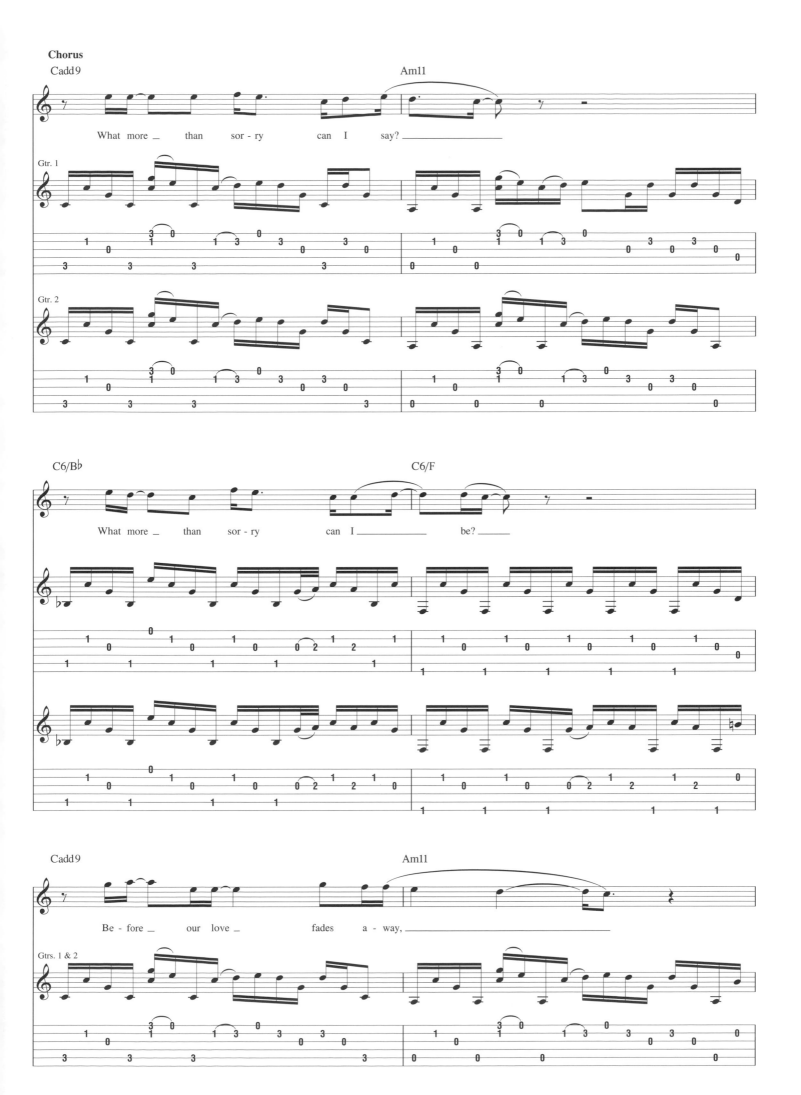

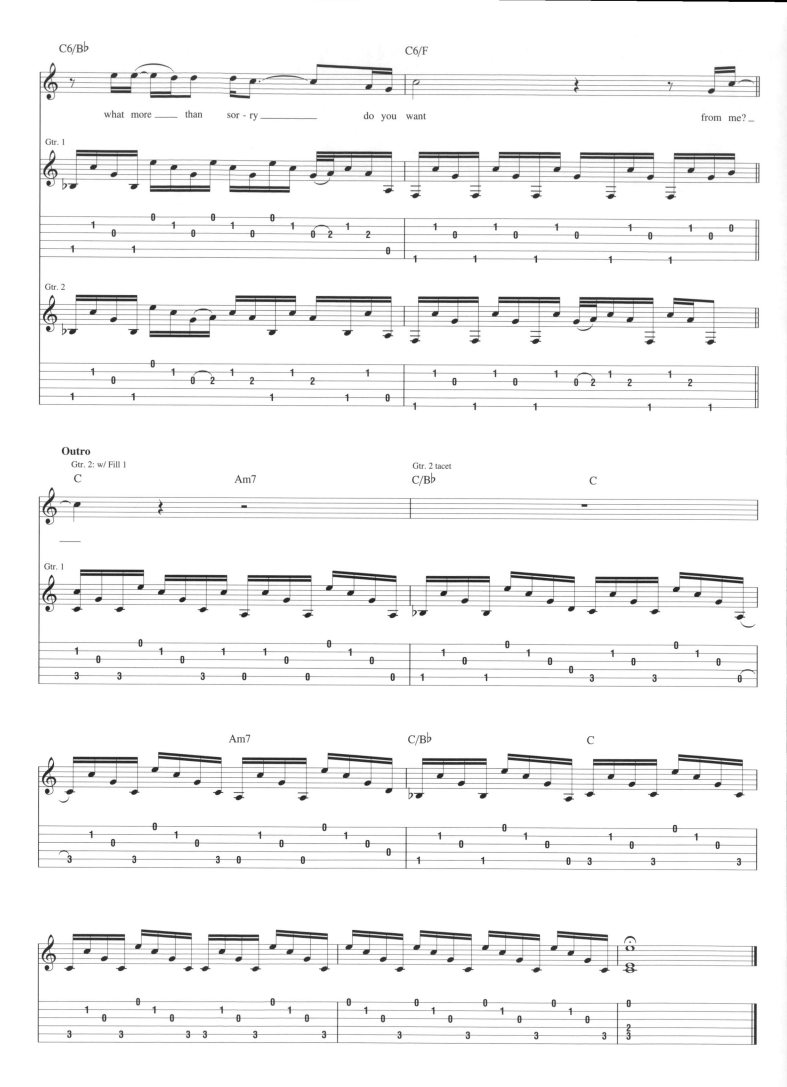

Cryin' Won't Help You Now

Words and Music by Ben Harper

Intro
Moderately slow ♩ = 66

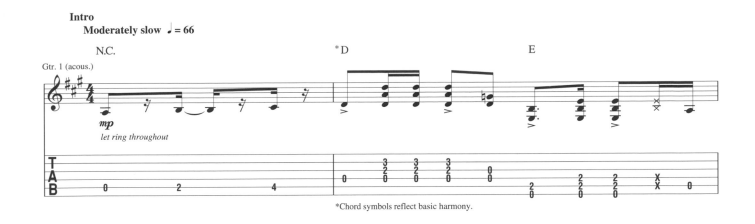

*Chord symbols reflect basic harmony.

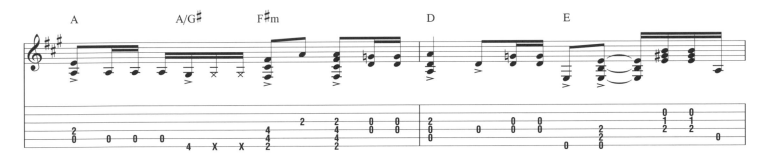

1. Sit __ there and call __ me a li - ar and a cheat.
2. Now __ your po - ets __ have all put down their pens. __

I___ just wish you'd pin a rose on ___ me.
The on-ly___ songs to sing are those ___ sung a-gain.___

2nd time, Gtr. 2: w/ Rhy. Fill 1

Now you won't e-ven come out and take a bow.___
Lone-ly just does - n't look good ___ on ___ you some-how.

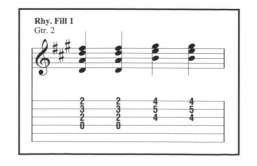

Rhy. Fill 1
Gtr. 2

Bridge

I ___ just keep _ on star - ing _____ in - to ___ the black _ eyes ____ of the

truth. We'll have _ to learn _ to live __ a - part ____ some - how.

Outro-Chorus

Cry - in' won't help _____ you now.
(Cry - in' won't help _____ you now. _____

Cry - in' won't help _____ you now.
Cry - in' won't help _____ you now. _____

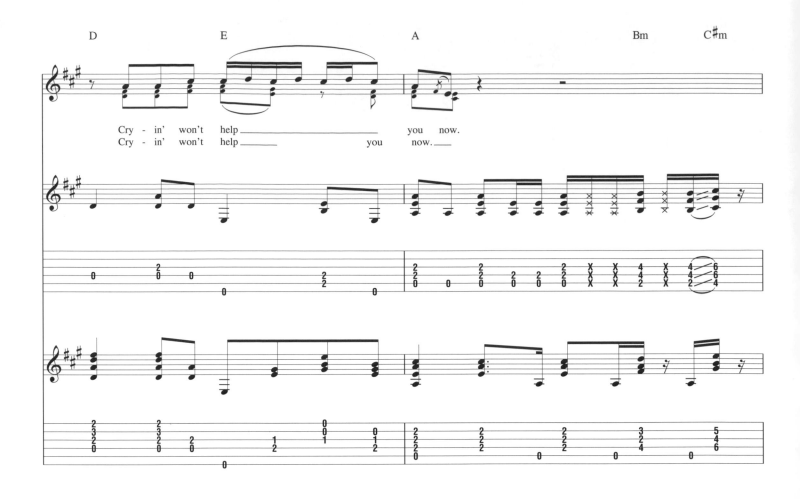

Cry - in' won't help _____ you now.
Cry - in' won't help _____ you now. _____

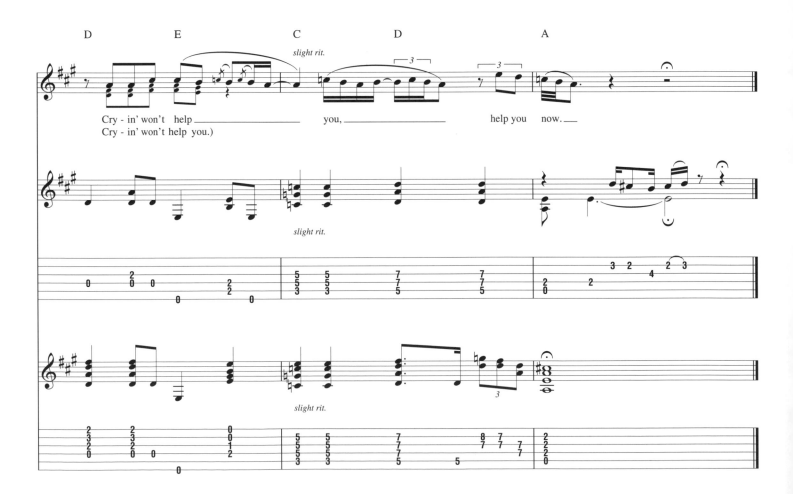

Cry - in' won't help _____ you, _____ help you now. _____
Cry - in' won't help you.)

Happy Everafter in Your Eyes

Words and Music by Ben Harper

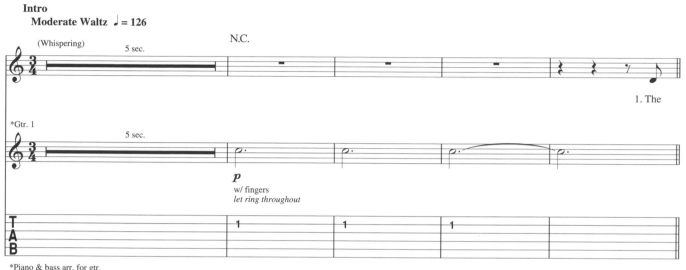

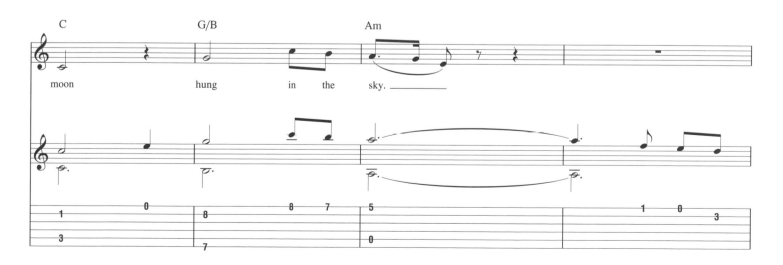

Verse

leave   you   to   go   to   heav - en.   I   car - ry   you

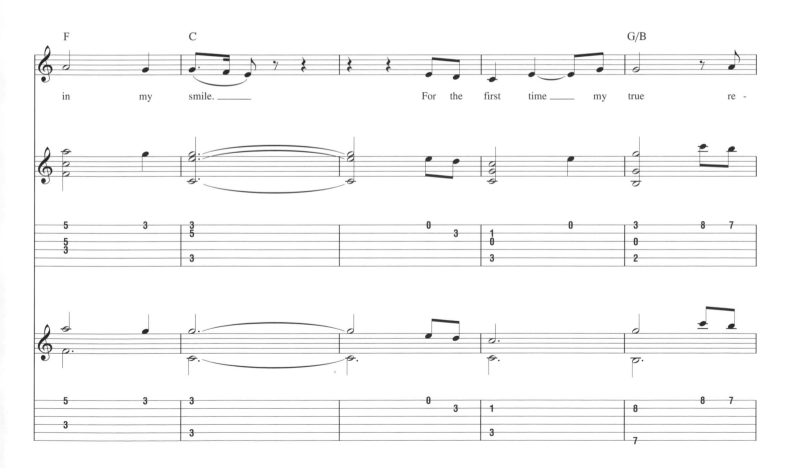

in   my   smile. _____   For the   first   time _____   my   true   re -

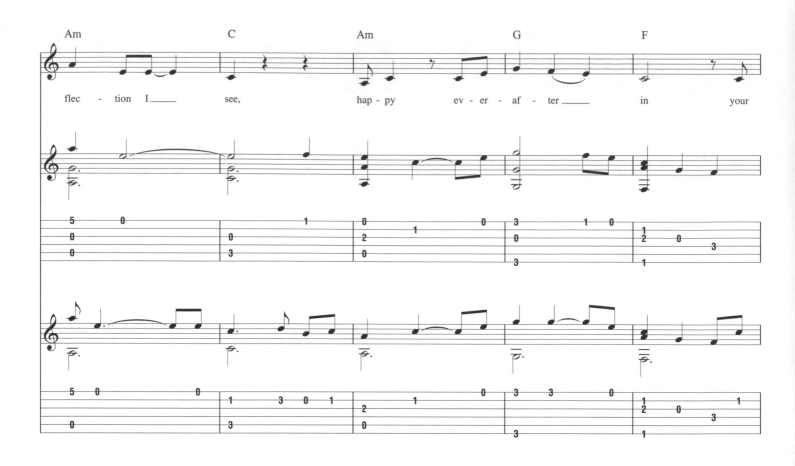

flec - tion I____ see, hap - py ev - er - af - ter ____ in your

eyes. Hap - py ev - er - af - ter is in your __ eyes.

Bridge

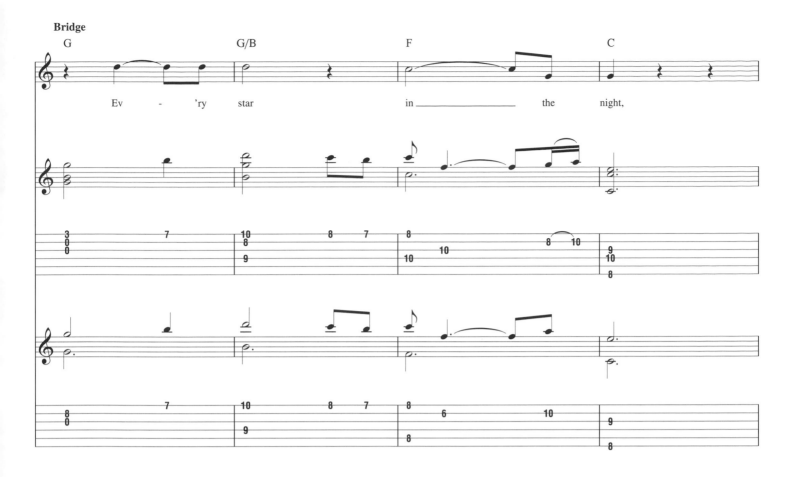

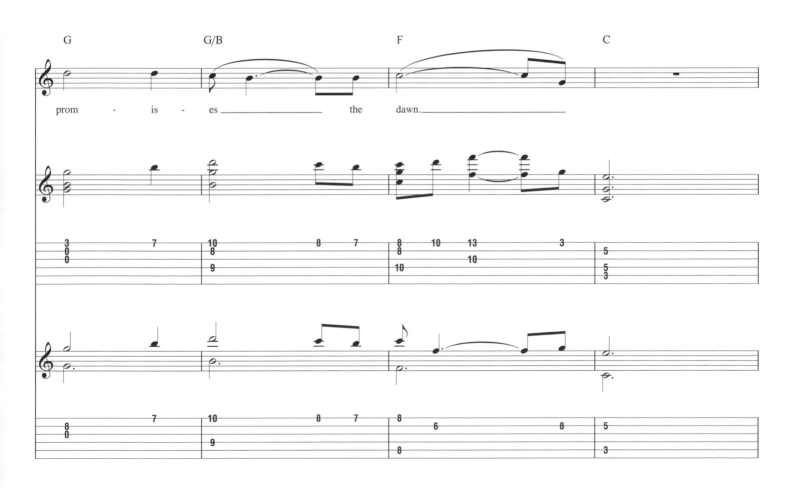

74

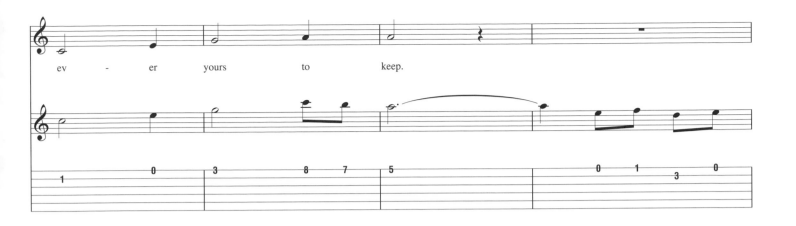

ev - er yours to keep.

Wake up ev - 'ry day with a dream, and

hap - py ev - er - af - ter _____ in your eyes. _____ Hap - py ev - er-

Gtr. 2

Gtr. 1

af - ter _____ is in your eyes. _____

76

Better Way

Words and Music by Ben Harper

Open E5 tuning, up 1/2 step:
(low to high) F-C-F-F-C-F

Intro
Moderately ♩ = 120

Spoken: One, two, one, two, three...

Play 3 times

*Gtr. 1
Rhy. Fig. 1   End Rhy. Fig. 1

E5

*Sitar arr. for gtr.

Verse

1st time, Gtr. 1: w/ Rhy. Fig. 1 (4 times)
2nd time, Gtr. 1: w/ Rhy. Fig. 1 (7 times)
3rd time, Gtr. 1: w/ Rhy. Fig. 1 (5 times)

E5

1. I'm a liv-ing sun-set, light-ning in my bones. ___ Push me to the edge but my will is stone. ___ I ___
2. Fools will be fools and wise will be wise. ___ But I will look this world straight in the eyes. ___ I ___
3. What good is a man who won't take a stand? ___ What good is a cyn-ic with no bet-ter plan? ___ I ___

*D   A   E   1.

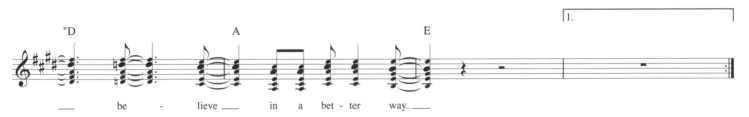

___ be - lieve ___ in a bet - ter way. ___

*Chord symbols reflect overall harmony.

2.   D   A   E

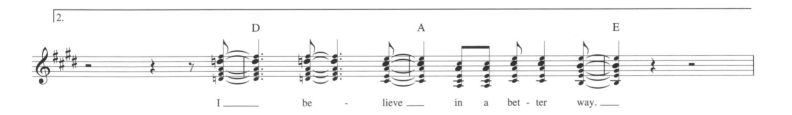

I ___ be - lieve ___ in a bet - ter way. ___

3.   D   A

Bkgd. Voc.: w/ Voc. ad lib.

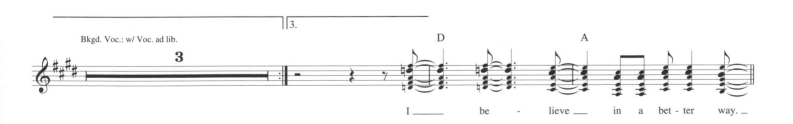

I ___ be - lieve ___ in a bet - ter way. ___

Guitar Solo

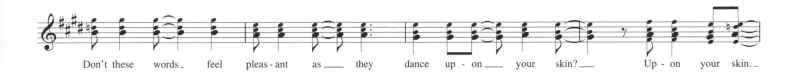

Don't these words_ feel pleas-ant as ___ they dance up-on ___ your skin? ___ Up-on your skin._

___ Up - on your skin. ___ Up - on your skin. ___ Up - on your skin. ___

Interlude
Gtr. 1: w/ Rhy. Fig. 1 (2 times)
E5

Verse
Gtr. 1: w/ Rhy. Fig. 1 (4 times)
E5

4. Re - al - i - ty is sharp, it cuts at me like a knife. ___

Ev -'ry-one I know is in the fight of their life. ___ I ___ be - lieve ___ in a bet-ter way.

Verse
Gtr. 1: w/ Rhy. Fig. 1 (7 times)
E   E5

5.Take your face out of your hands_ and clear your eyes. __ You have a

D   A

right to your dreams_ and don't be de-nied. I ___ be - lieve ___ in a bet-ter way._

E   D   A

___ I ___ be - lieve ___ in a bet-ter way._

E   D   A

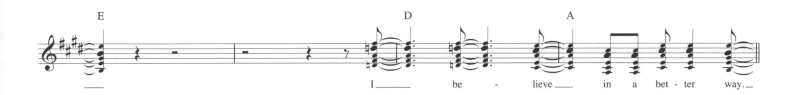

___ I ___ be - lieve ___ in a bet-ter way._

Outro

Gtr. 1: w/ Rhy. Fig. 1 (2 times)

*Viola arr. for gtr.

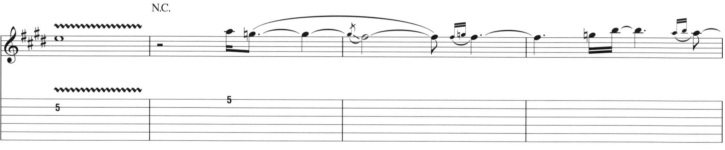

N.C.

Gtr. 3 tacet
(Drums)

Both Sides of the Gun

Words and Music by Ben Harper

*Gtr. 1 (clean tone) w/ wah-wah; Gtr. 2 (acous.)

**Chord symbols reflect basic harmony.

1. Liv-ing these days is mak-ing me ner - vous. Ar - cha - ic doc - trine no long-er serve _ us. Now we're

left as si - lent wit - ness - es. ___ We don't know _ quite what _ this is ___

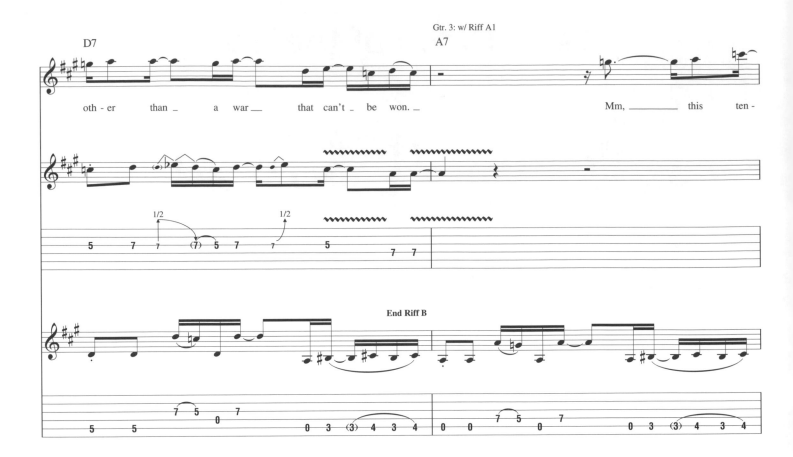

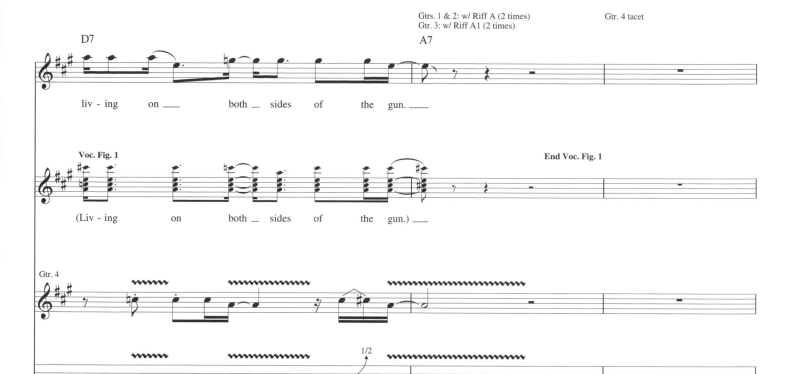

liv - ing   on ____   both ___ sides   of   the   gun. ____

(Liv - ing   on ____   both ___ sides   of   the   gun.) ____

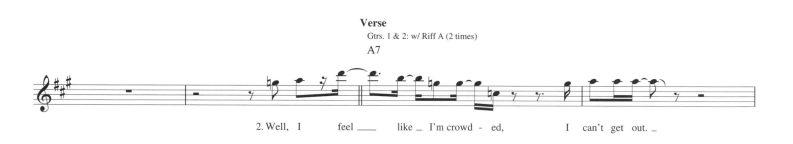

2. Well, I   feel ____   like _ I'm crowd - ed,   I   can't get out. _

World keeps _ on   fill - ing ____   me   up   with doubt. _   When you're trapped _   you got ___ no   voice. _

one foot in the grave _____ and the oth - er on the flag. _____

Gtrs. 1 & 2: w/ Riff C
E7

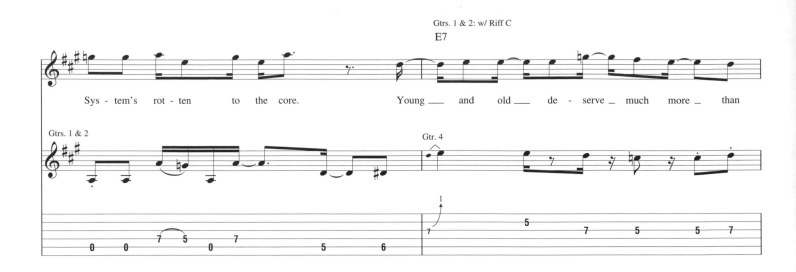

Sys - tem's rot - ten to the core. Young _____ and old _____ de - serve _____ much more _____ than

Gtrs. 1 & 2

Gtr. 4

D7   A7

Gtr. 3: w/ Riff A1

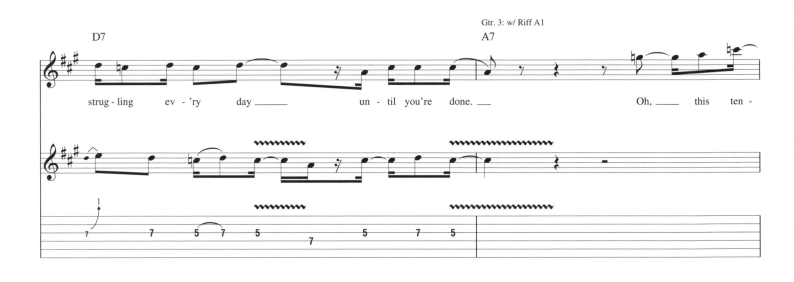

strug - ling ev -'ry day _____ un - til you're done. _____ Oh, _____ this ten -

Gtrs. 1 & 2: w/ Riff C
E7

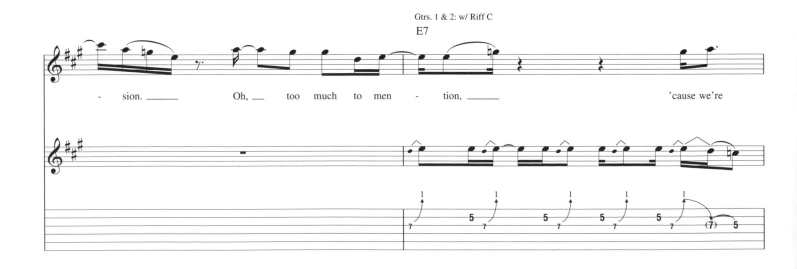

- sion. _____ Oh, _____ too much to men - tion, _____ 'cause we're

liv-ing on — both — sides of the gun. — Mm, — ten - sion, oh, — I — can't men-

(Both sides of the gun.) —

- tion. — We're liv - ing on — both — sides of the gun. — Oh, — liv-ing on

both sides, oh — liv - ing on both sides. — Broth - er,

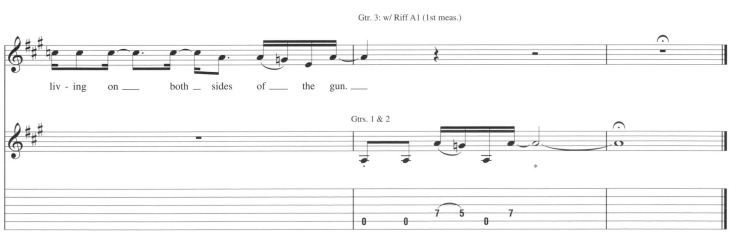

liv - ing on — both — sides of — the gun. —

*Gtr. 1 rocks wah-wah pedal till end.

Engraved Invitation

Words and Music by Ben Harper

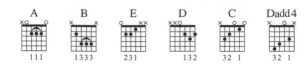

Gtr. 1: Open E tuning:
(low to high) E-B-E-G♯-B-E

Intro
Moderately ♩ = 116

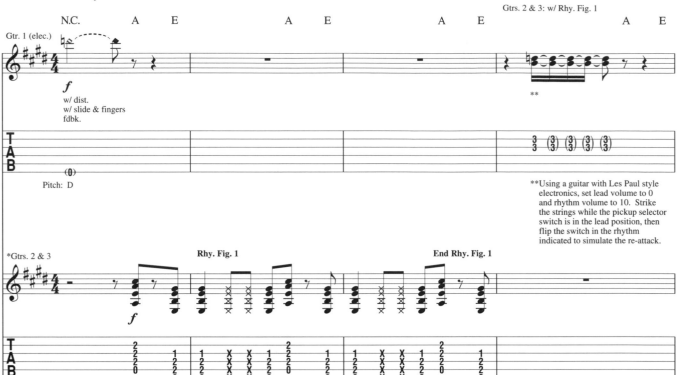

*Gtr. 2 (acous.); Gtr. 3 (elec.) w/ dist. Composite arrangement

**Using a guitar with Les Paul style electronics, set lead volume to 0 and rhythm volume to 10. Strike the strings while the pickup selector switch is in the lead position, then flip the switch in the rhythm indicated to simulate the re-attack.

𝄋 Verse

Gtr. 1 tacet
Gtrs. 2 & 3: w/ Rhy. Fig. 1 (3 1/2 times)
3rd time, Gtr. 4 tacet

1. I wish I was a thought. I'd run all through your mind ____ and come out be-ing ev-'ry-thing you
   wish I could yell sor-ry loud-er than I screamed ____ all of those oth-er things I
   sun's a moon that warms you, the moon's a sun with no heat. The sky a-bove is to re-mind you

ev-er tried to find. Life's the long-est pic-ture you're ev-er gon-na take. ____ Love's the long-est prom-ise that you're
said but did-n't mean. Some days I'm the Lord's ser-vant, some days I'm Sa-tan's pawn. ____ Some days I just wish the voic-es in
what's un-der your feet. This life's not big e-nough to fit our love in-side, ____ 'cause I re-mem-ber you from heav-en

*Slide positioned halfway between the 8th & 9th frets.

89

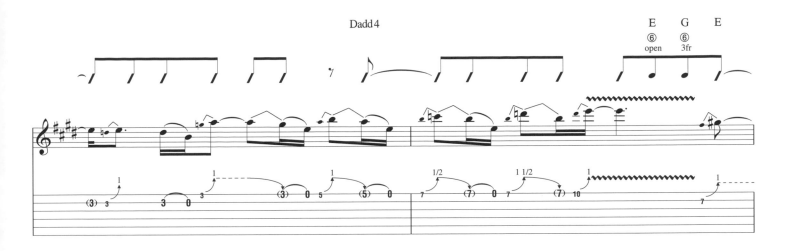

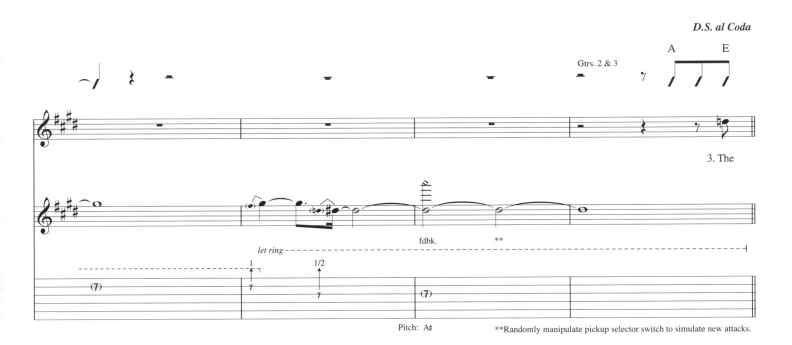

Pitch: A♯   **Randomly manipulate pickup selector switch to simulate new attacks.

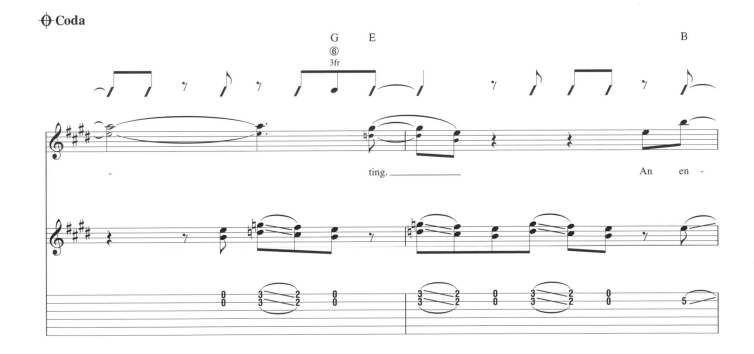

graved   in -   vi -   ta -

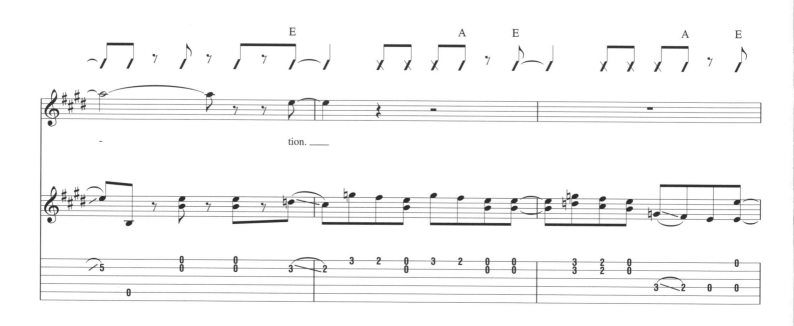

tion. ___

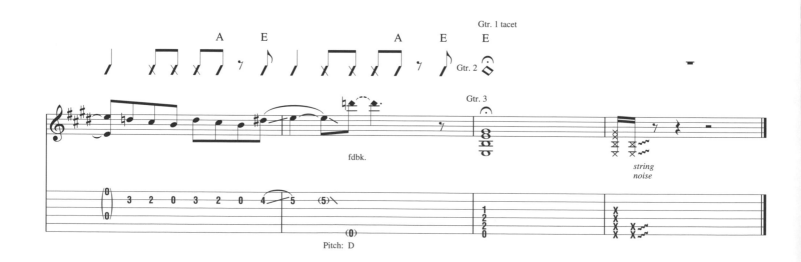

Black Rain

Words and Music by Ben Harper and Jason Yates

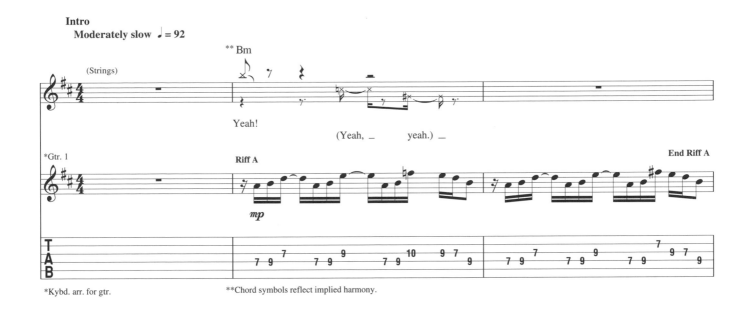

Can't af-ford a gal-lon of gas-o-line. With your
-pa-thy for us, still I cry for you.

End Riff B

Gtr. 1: w/ Riff B

use-less de-grees and your con-tra-ry sta-tis-tics, this
You may kill the rev-o-lu-tion-ar-y, but the rev-

Rhy. Fig. 1

*Gtr. 2

mp

*Strings arr. for gtr.

1.

gov-ern-ment busi-ness is straight up sa-dis-tic. And this
-o-lu-tion you can nev-er bur-

End Rhy. Fig. 1

Chorus

Gtr. 2 tacet

Bm   A   D   E

black rain, whoa, said a black rain is gon-na

Gtr. 1

Coda

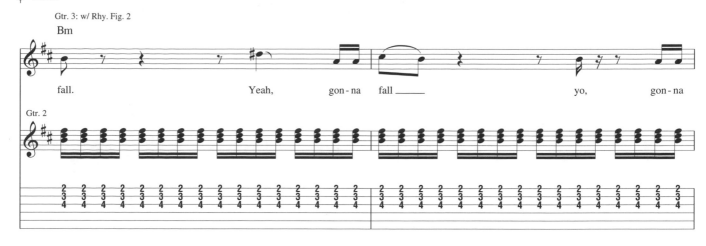

fall.   Yeah,   gon-na   fall _____   yo,   gon-na

fall, _____   one and   all. _____

Gather 'Round the Stone

Words and Music by Ben Harper

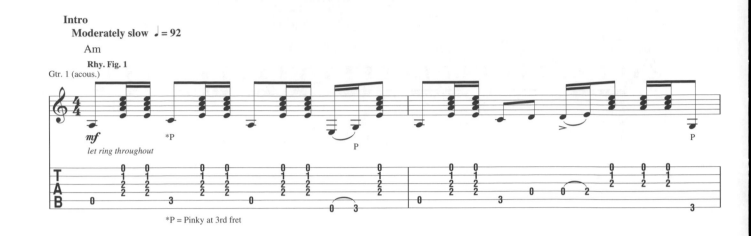

*P = Pinky at 3rd fret

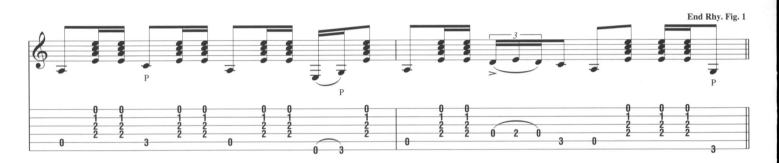

Chorus

Gtr. 1: w/ Rhy. Fig. 1

Hey, hey, hey, hey, _ gath-er 'round _ the stone. Hey, _ hey, _ hey, hey, _ gath-er 'round the stone. _
{ 1. You're
{ 4. Old

Verse

too   young _ to know _____   that you're   too   young _ to go. _   There's   no
2. Ash- es   from the un-   fin-ished   life   are   all _____ that's left _   in a
men who send _   chil- dren   off   to die _____   in   vain,   they will

Rhy. Fig. 2

Gtr. 1

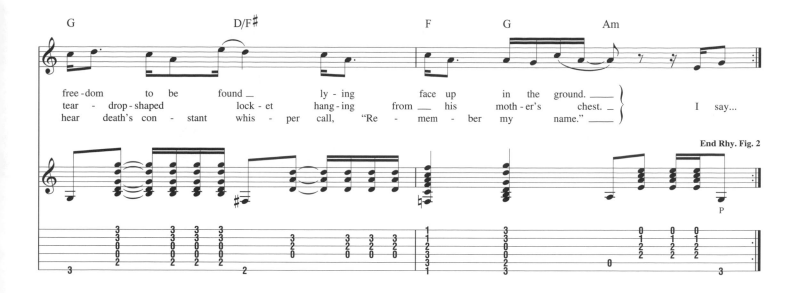

freedom to be found lying face up in the ground. ___
teardrop-shaped locket hanging from his mother's chest. ___ I say...
hear death's constant whisper call, "Remember my name." ___

End Rhy. Fig. 2

Chorus

1st time, Gtr. 1: w/ Rhy. Fig. 1 (1 1/2 times)
2nd time, Gtrs. 1 & 3: w/ Rhy. Fig. 1 (2 1/2 times)

Hey, hey, hey, hey, gather 'round ___ the stone. ___ Hey, ___ hey, ___ hey, hey, ___ gather 'round the stone. ___ Say

Voc. Fig. 1   **End Voc. Fig. 1**

(Hey, hey, hey, hey, gather 'round ___ the stone. Hey, hey, hey, hey, gather 'round ___ the stone.)

1st time, Bkgd. Voc.: w/ Voc. Fig. 1
2nd time, Bkgd. Voc.: w/ Voc. Fig. 1 (2 times)

hey,
Hey,   hey, ___ hey, hey, ___ gather 'round ___ the stone. ___ I say,

To Coda ⊕

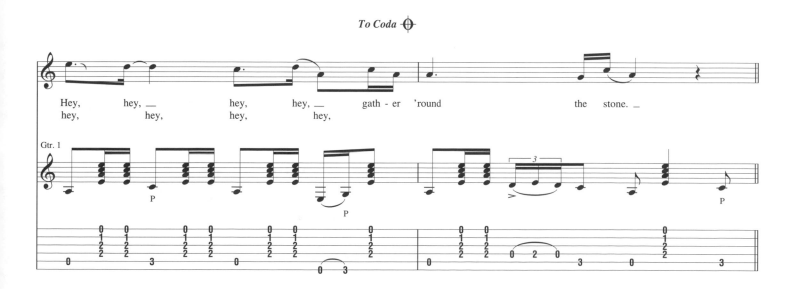

Hey, hey, ___ hey, hey, ___ gather 'round the stone. ___
hey, hey, hey, hey,

Gtr. 1

Guitar Solo

*Gtr. 3 (acous.) played **mf**; Composite arrangement

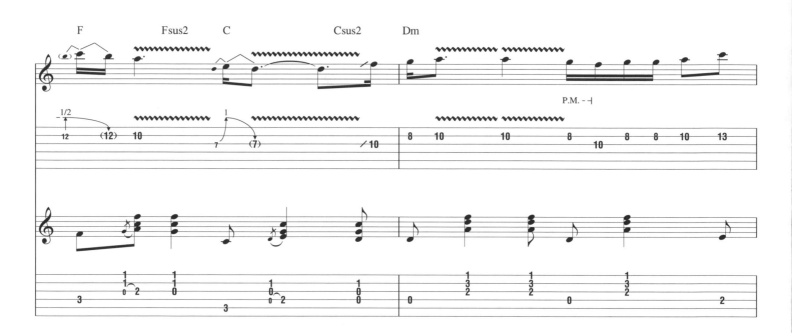

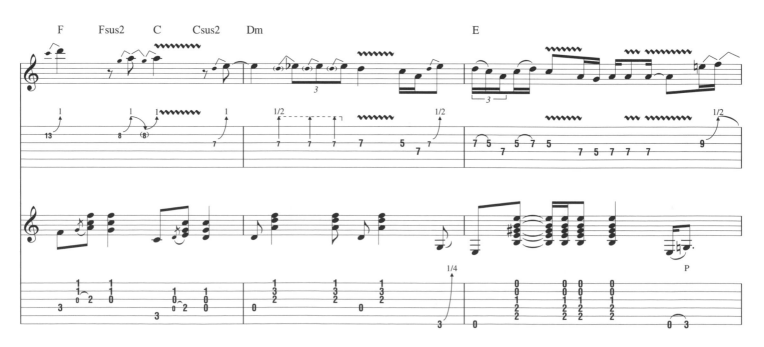

Gtr. 1: w/ Rhy. Fig. 1
Gtr. 3 tacet
Gtr. 2 tacet

Am

3. You

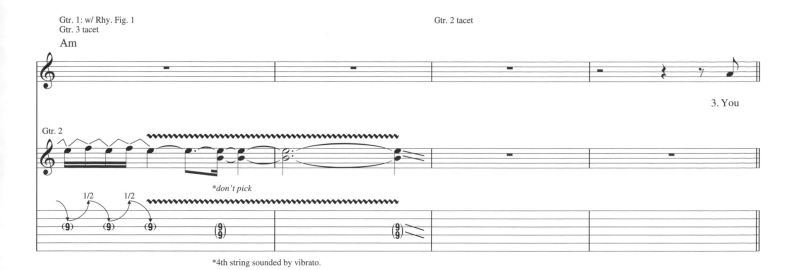

*4th string sounded by vibrato.

Verse
Gtr. 1: w/ Rhy. Fig. 2
Am

whip the back __ of free - dom __ 'till it bleeds an oil __ stream, __ then you

D.S. al Coda
(no repeat)

G   D/F#   F   G   Am

sail __ down __ up - on __ it in your kill - ing ma - chine. ___ I said...

Coda

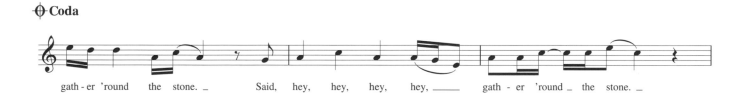

gath - er 'round the stone. _ Said, hey, hey, hey, hey, ____ gath - er 'round _ the stone. _

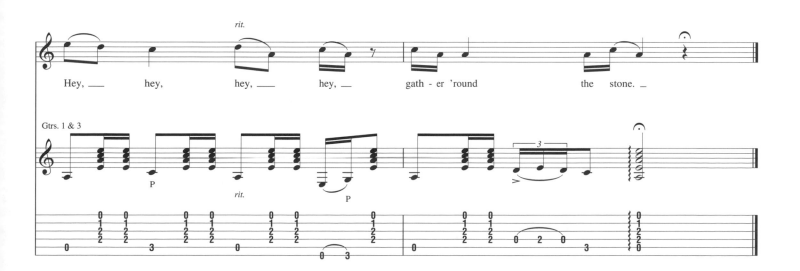

Hey, ___ hey, ___ hey, ___ hey, __ gath - er 'round the stone. _

Gtrs. 1 & 3

Please Don't Talk About Murder While I'm Eating

Words and Music by Ben Harper

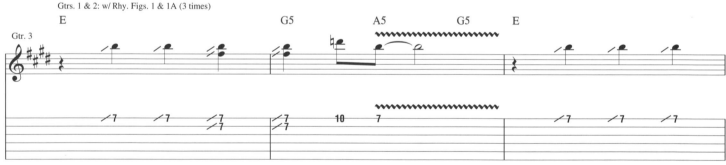

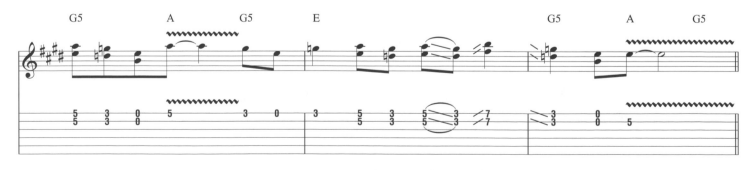

Verse

Gtrs. 1 & 2: w/ Rhy. Fig. 1 (4 times)

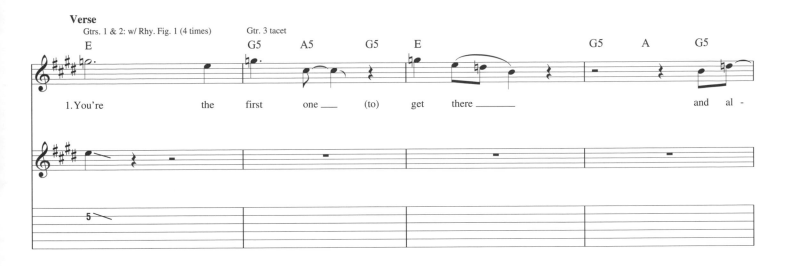

1. You're the first one ___ (to) get there ___ and al -

- ways ___ the last one ___ to leave.

You're the first one ___ to chuck - le

Rhy. Fig. 2

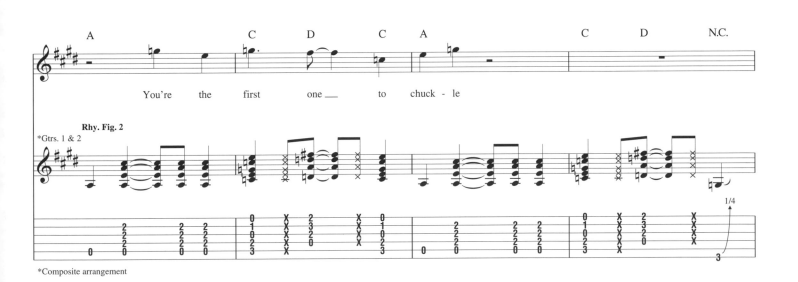

*Gtrs. 1 & 2

*Composite arrangement

but the last ___ one ___ to grieve. ___ I

know all too well the world___ takes a dai - ly beat - ing. But

Chorus

please don't talk a - bout mur - der while___ I'm eat - ing.

2. You

Chorus

Guitar Solo

108

Outro-Chorus

Gtrs. 1 & 2: w/ Rhy. Figs. 1 & 1A (5 times)

Please — don't talk a - bout — mur - der while — I'm eat - ing.

Gtr. 3

steady gliss.

Please — don't talk a - bout — mur - der while I'm eat - ing.

Gtrs. 1 & 3

Let's not talk — a - bout mur - der while — I'm eat - ing.

Free time

fdbk.

109

Get It Like You Like It

Words and Music by Ben Harper

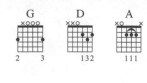

*Bass plays F♯.

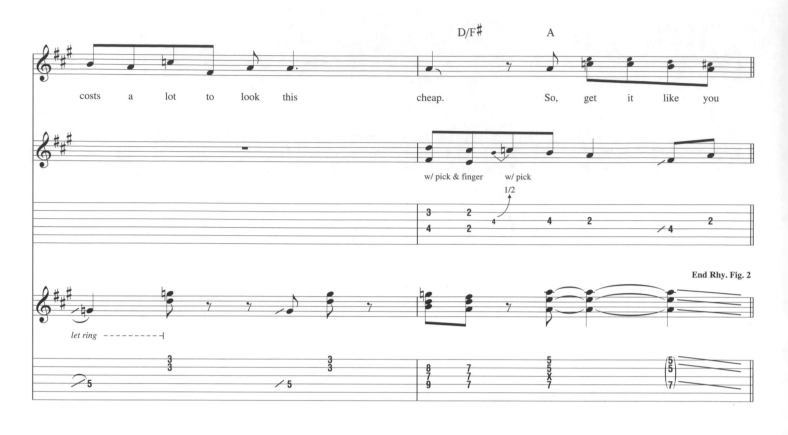

costs a lot to look this cheap. So, get it like you

End Rhy. Fig. 2

𝄋 Chorus

Gtr. 1: w/ Rhy. Fig. 1 (1st 3 meas.)
Gtr. 3: w/ Rhy. Fig. 1A (2 times)

Gtr. 1: w/ Rhy. Fill 1

like it. Get it like you like it._____ Get it like you

Gtr. 2 Rhy. Fig. 3

End Rhy. Fig. 3

To Coda ⊕

Gtr. 1: w/ Rhy. Fig. 1
2nd time, Gtr. 2: w/ Rhy. Fig. 3

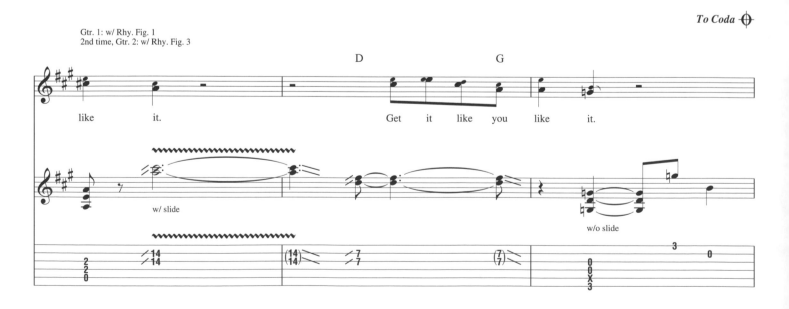

like it. Get it like you like it.

w/ slide

w/o slide

112

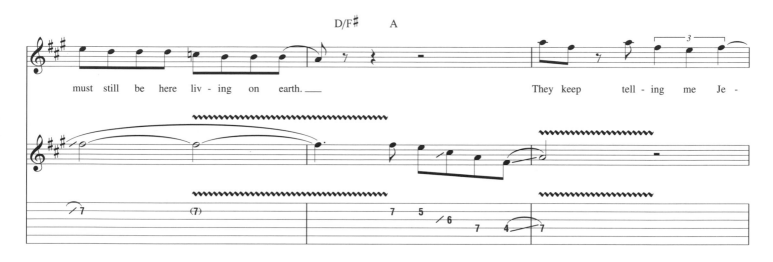

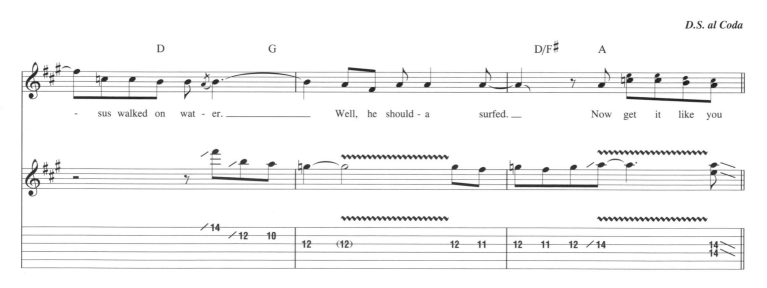

113

But John - ny Da - mon swung a bat.

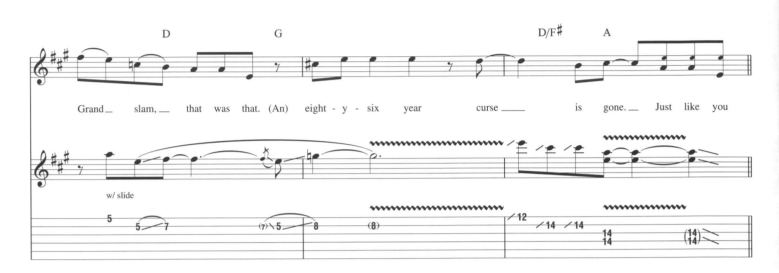

Grand__ slam,__ that was that. (An) eight - y - six year curse ____ is gone. __ Just like you

Chorus
Gtr. 1: w/ Riff A (2 times)
Gtr. 2: w/ Rhy. Fig. 3 (1 3/4 times)
Gtr. 3: w/ Rhy. Fig. 1A (2 times)
Gtr. 4: w/ Riff A

like it. Get it like you like it. Get it like you

like it. __
(like it.)

Get it like you like it.

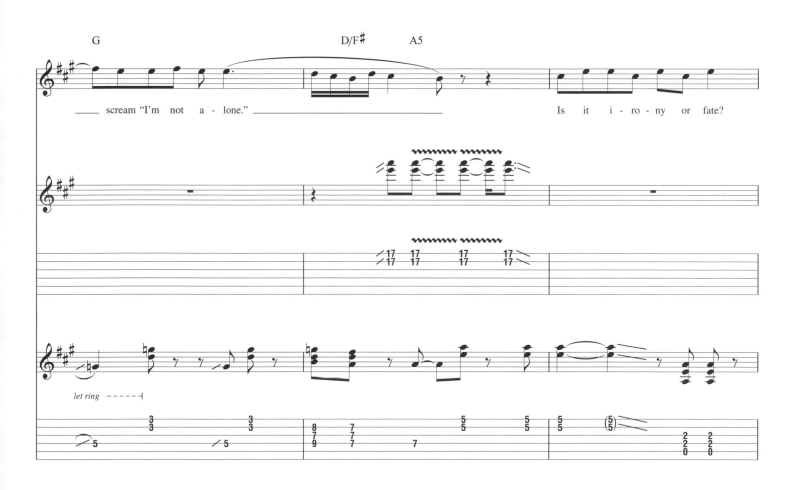

*Bass plays D.

Chorus

Gtrs. 1 & 3: w/ Rhy. Figs. 1 & 1A (4 times)

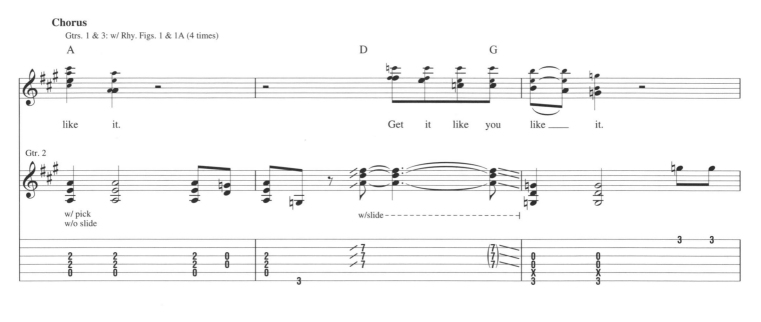

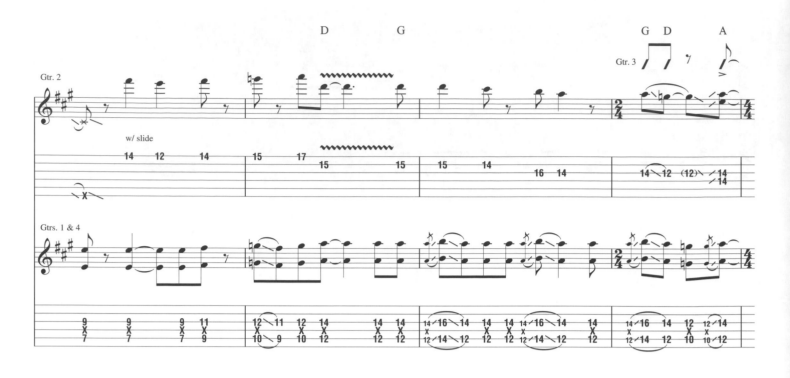

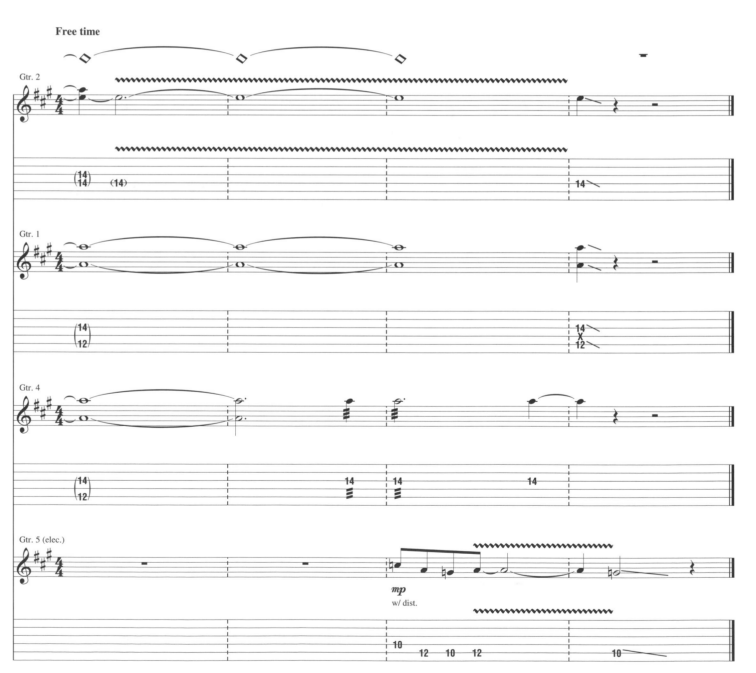

The Way You Found Me

Words and Music by Ben Harper

Gtr. 2: Open E5 tuning:
(low to high) E-B-E-E-B-E

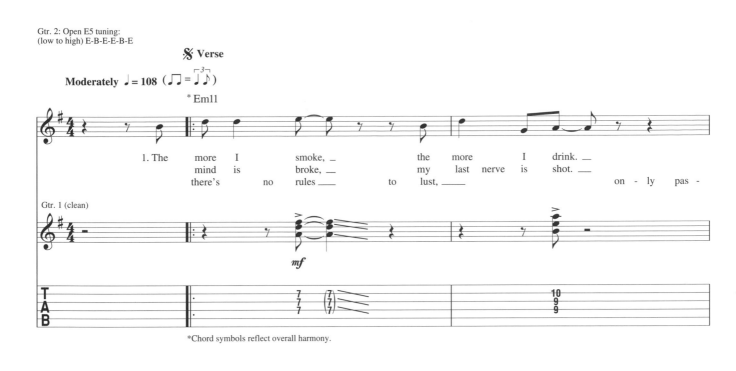

*Chord symbols reflect overall harmony.

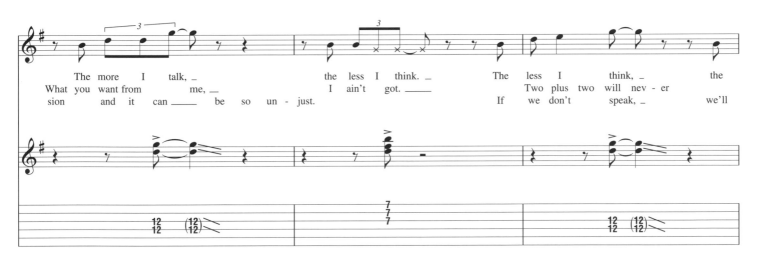

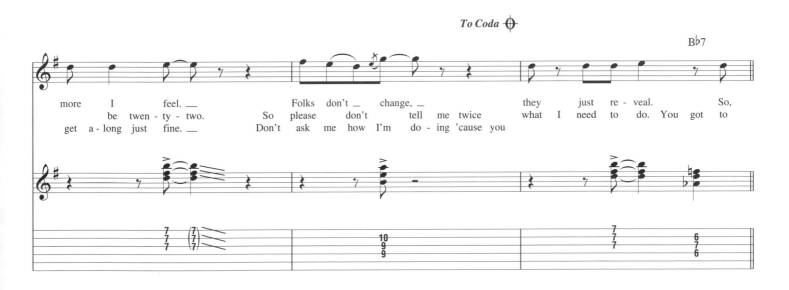

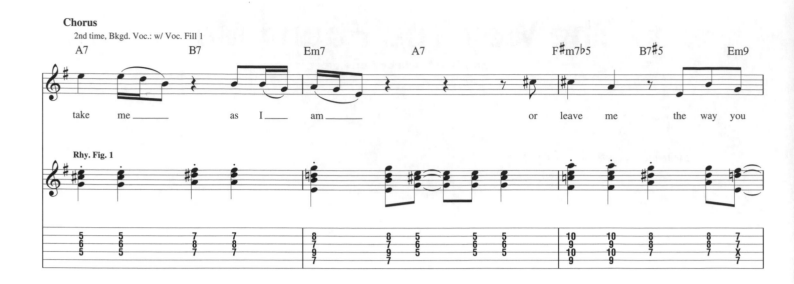

take me _____ as I _____ am _____ or leave me the way you

found _____ me, the way you found me, the way you found _____ me.

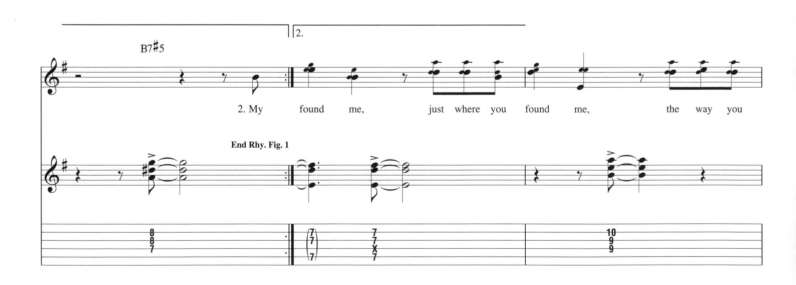

2. My found me, just where you found me, the way you

(Take me as I am. The way you...)

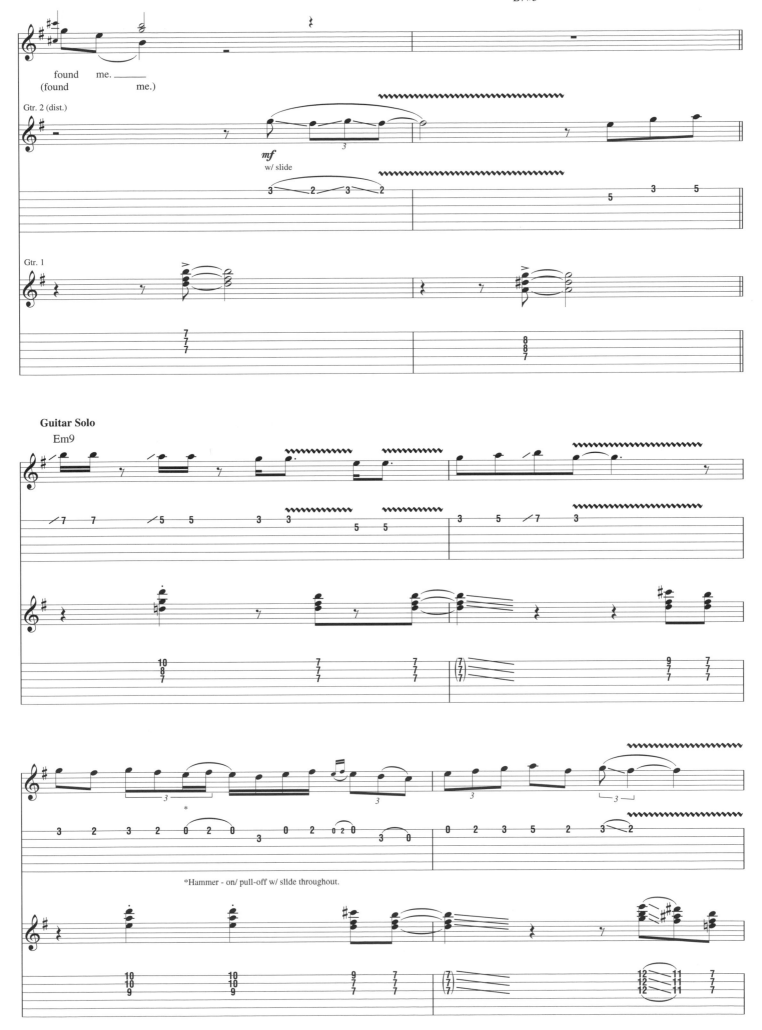

A9

Em9

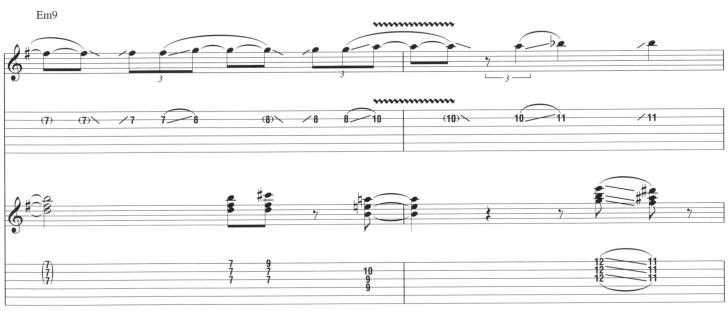

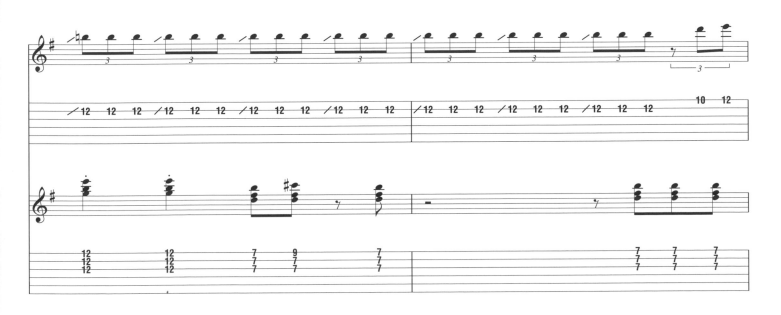

124

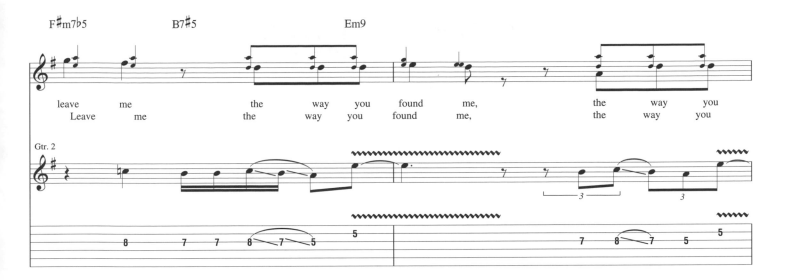

leave me   the way you found me,   the way you
Leave me   the way you found   me,   the way you

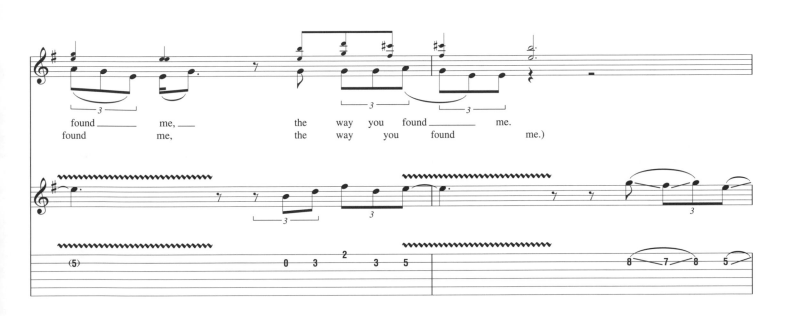

found _____ me, _____   the way you found _____ me.
found   me, _____   the way you found   me.)

Free time

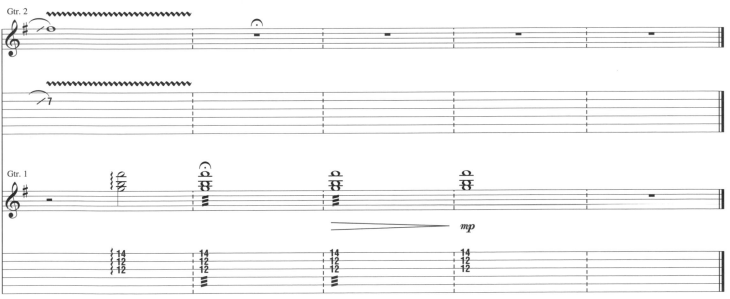

Serve Your Soul

Words and Music by Ben Harper

Gtrs. 1-4 & 7-10: Drop D tuning:
(low to high) D-A-D-G-B-E

Gtrs. 5, 6 & 11: Open D5 tuning:
(low to high) D-A-D-D↓-A-D

Intro
Slowly ♩ = 72

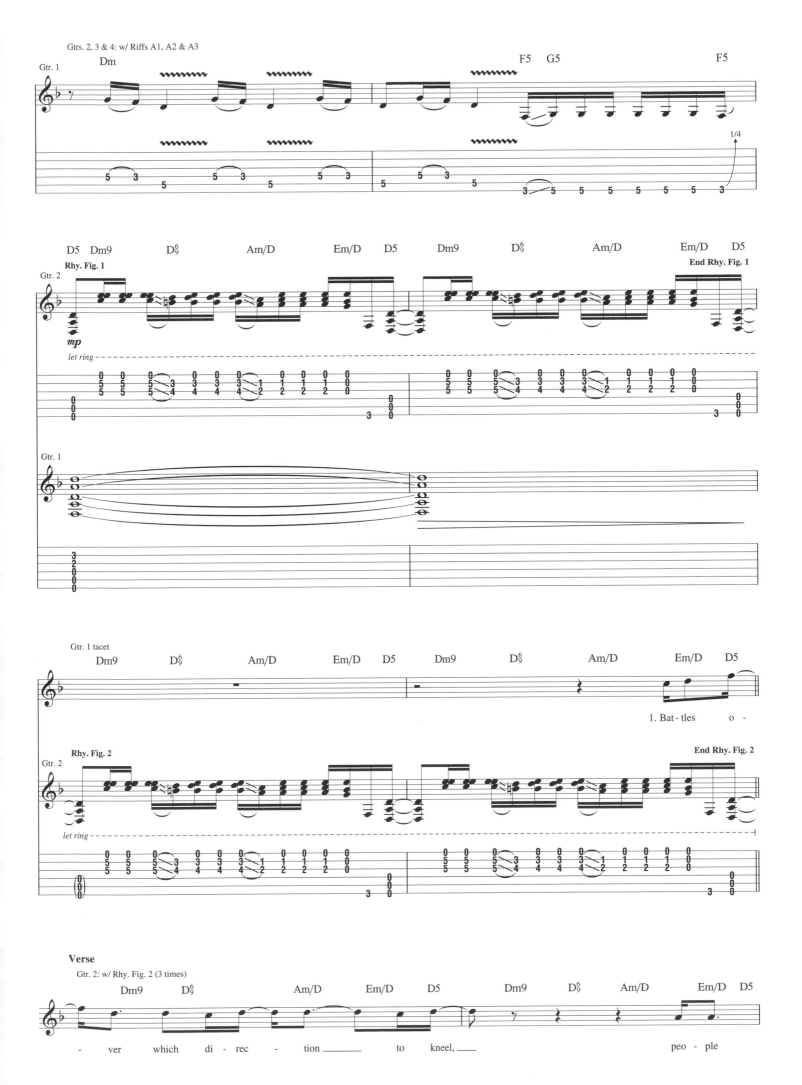

reach - ing out to touch ___ but for - get - ting ___ to feel. ___

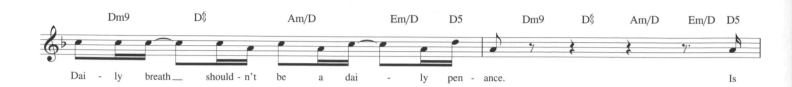

Dai - ly breath ___ should - n't be a dai - ly pen - ance. Is

that what you be - lieve, ___ or just ___ a life ___ sen - tence? I

Chorus

look in - to the mir - ror and I see ___ some - one ___ there I used to know. ___

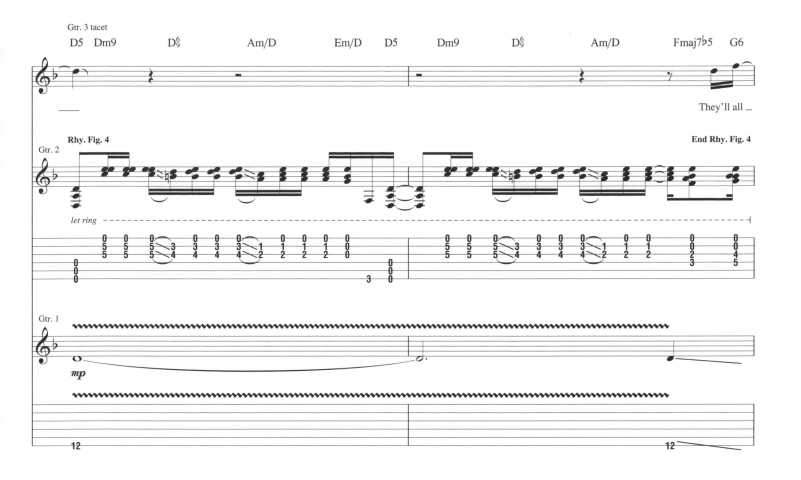

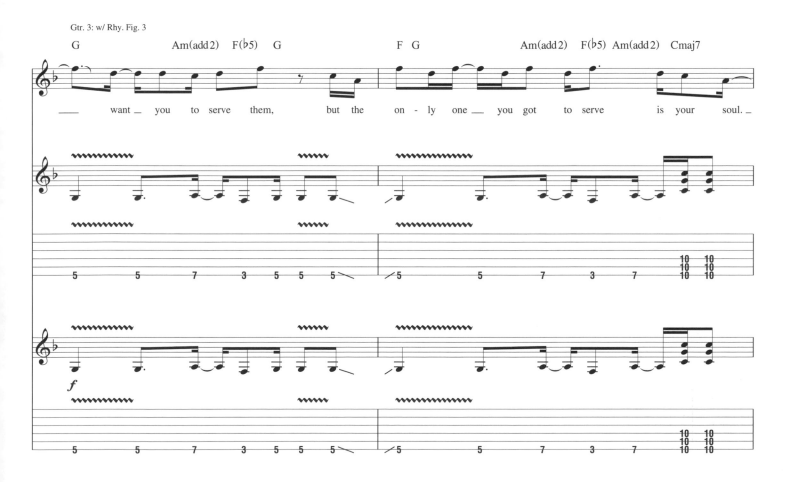

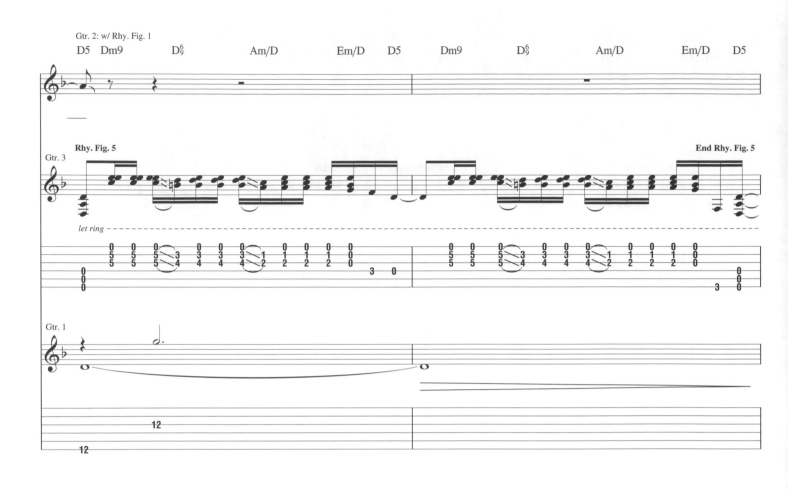

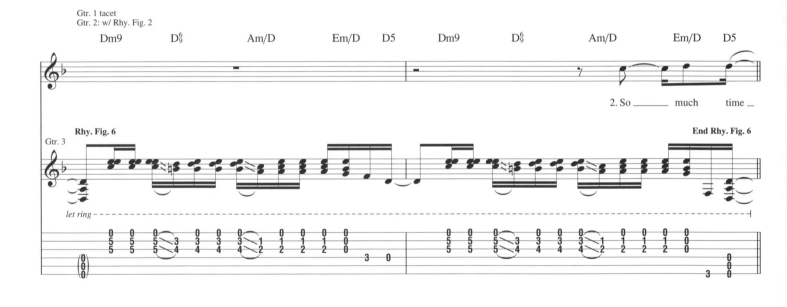

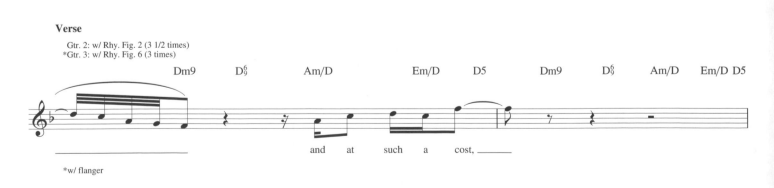

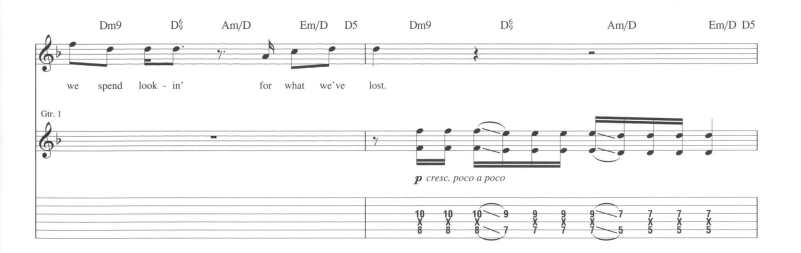

we spend look - in'   for what we've lost.

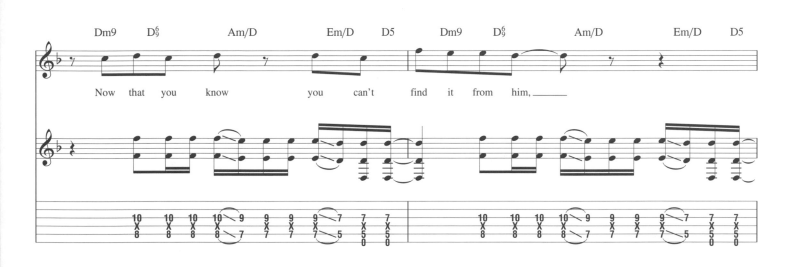

Now that you know   you can't   find it from him,_____

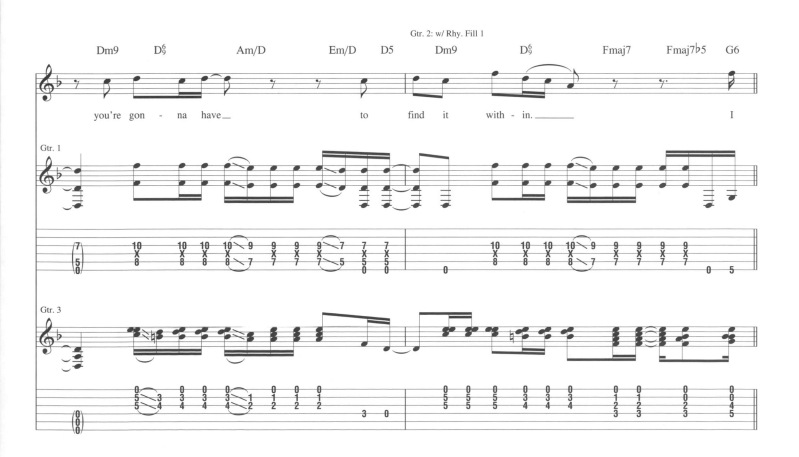

you're gon - na have__ to find it with - in._____ I

Chorus

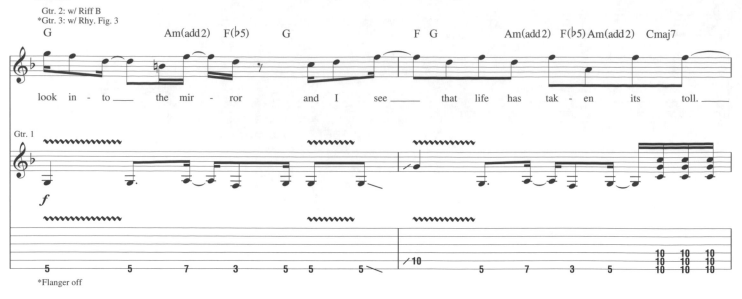

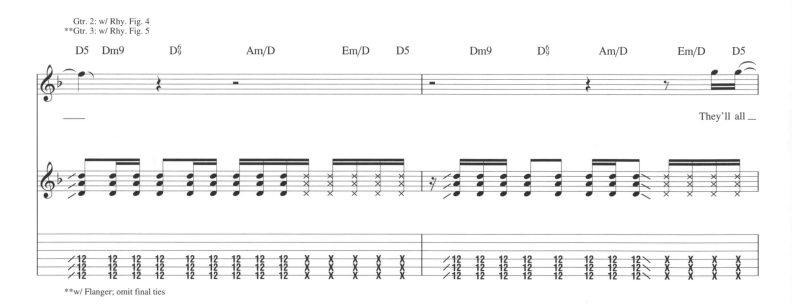

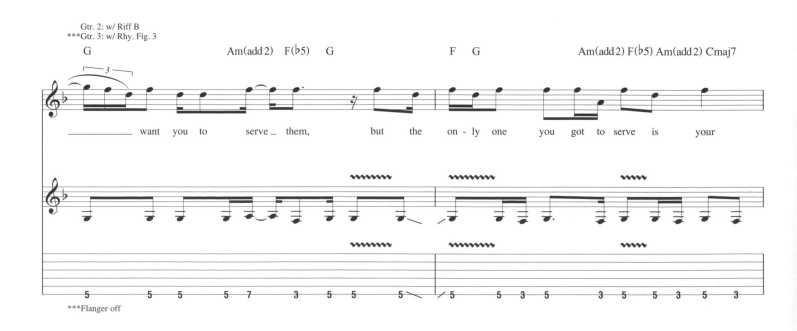

*Gtr. 2: w/ Rhy. Fig. 1
*Gtr. 3: w/ Rhy. Fig. 5

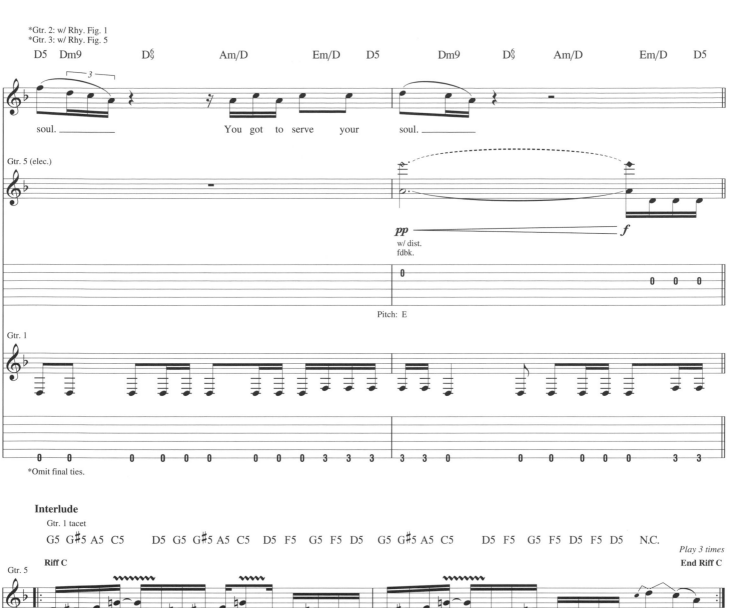

soul. _____ You got to serve your soul. _____

Gtr. 5 (elec.)

pp ——————— f
w/ dist.
fdbk.

Pitch: E

Gtr. 1

*Omit final ties.

Interlude
Gtr. 1 tacet

G5 G#5 A5 C5   D5 G5 G#5 A5 C5   D5 F5 G5 F5 D5   G5 G#5 A5 C5   D5 F5 G5 F5 D5 F5 D5 N.C.

Play 3 times

Gtr. 5   Riff C   End Riff C

Riff C1   End Riff C1
Gtr. 6 (elec.)

f
w/ dist.

Gtr. 6: w/ Riff C1

G5 G#5 A5 C5   D5 G5 G#5 A5 C5   D5 F5 G5 F5 D5   G5 G#5 A5 C5   D5 F5 G5 F5 D5 F5 D5 N.C.

Gtr. 5   Riff D   End Riff D

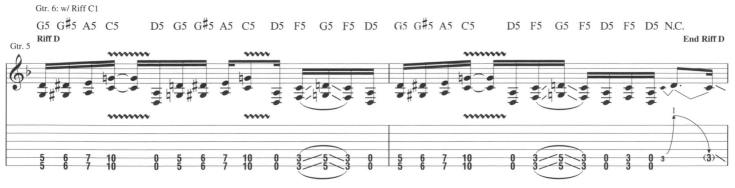

*Acous. gtrs. played **mp**.

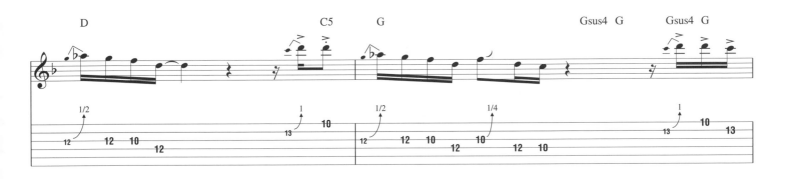

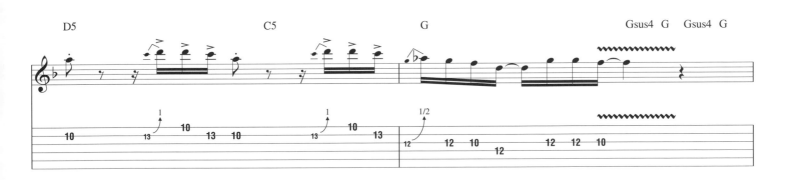

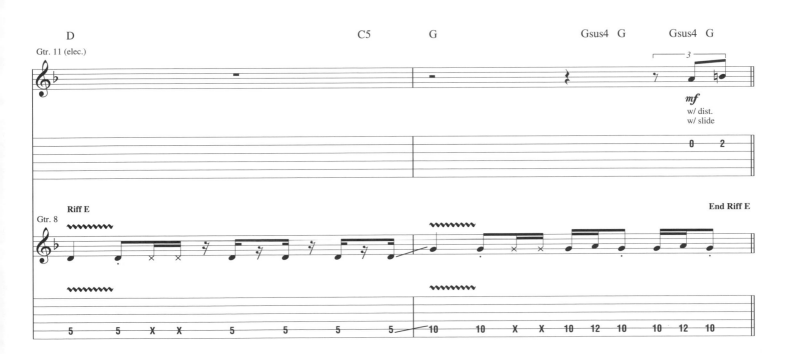

Guitar Solo

Gtr. 8: w/ Riff E (3 times)
Gtrs. 9 & 10: w/ Rhy. Fig. 7 (5 times)

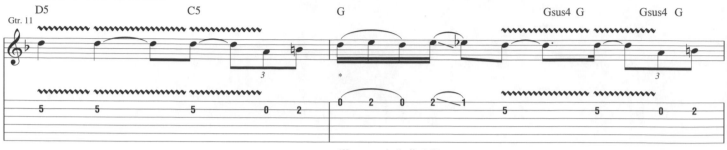

*Hammer-on/pull-off w/ slide.

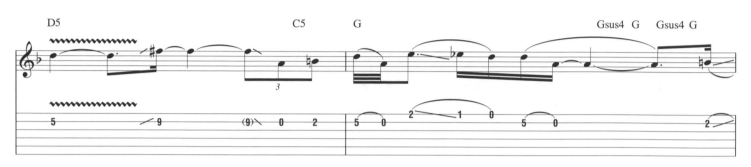

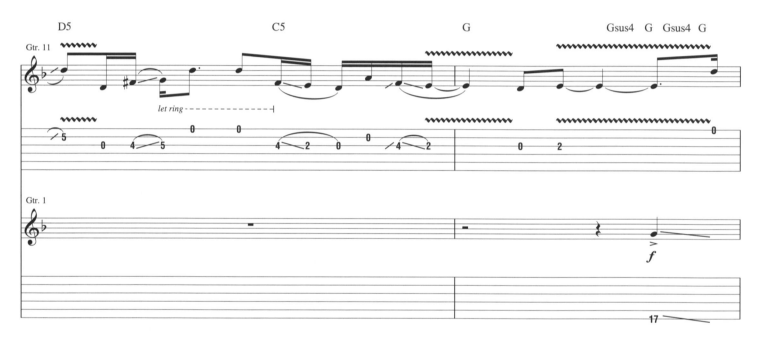

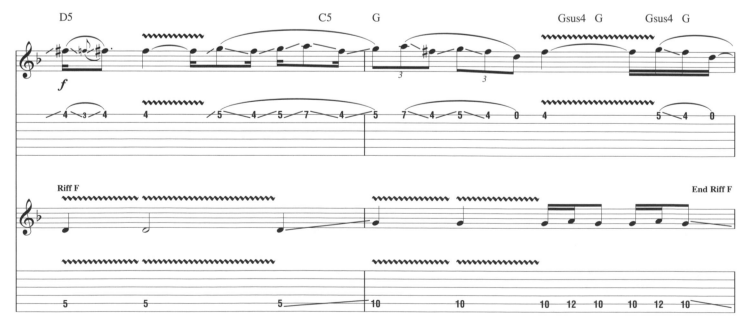

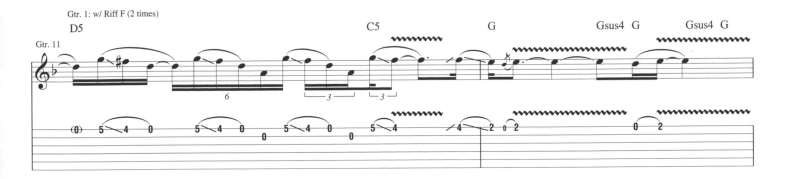

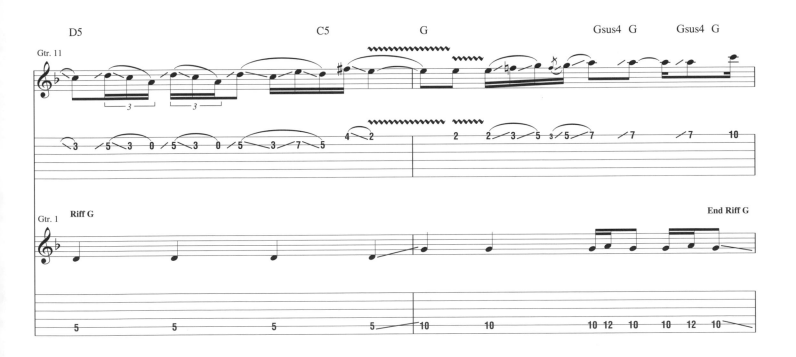

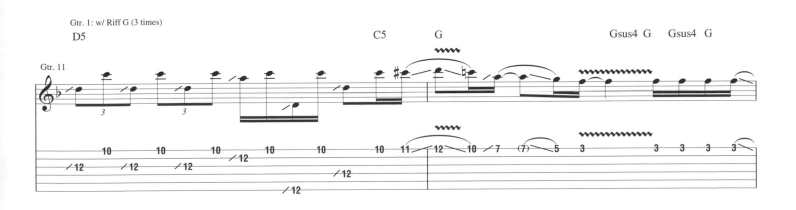

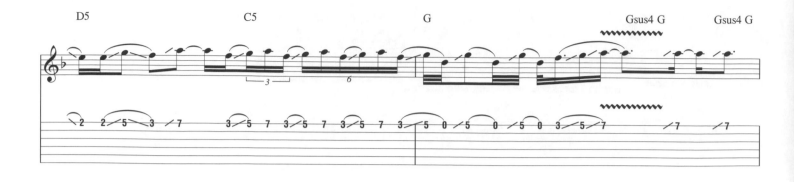

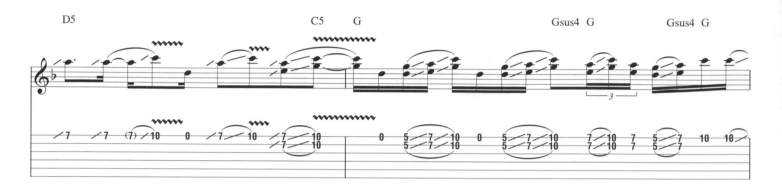

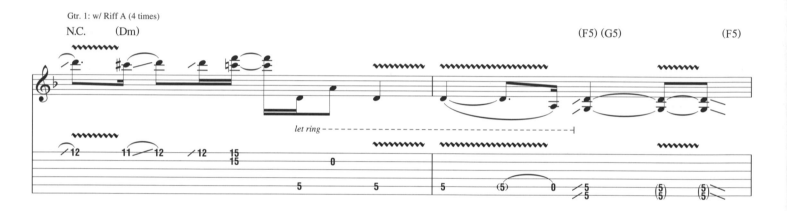

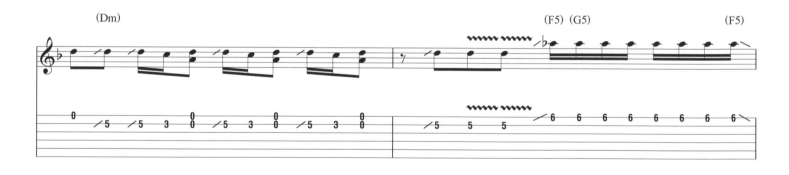

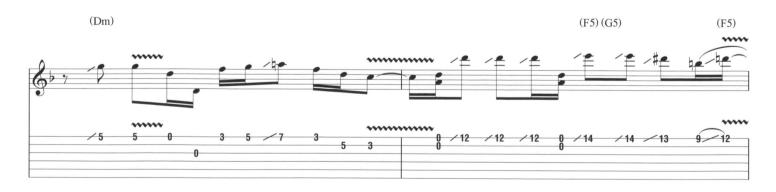

*Slide positioned halfway between 6th & 7th frets.

Verse

Gtr. 2: w/ Rhy. Fig. 1
Gtr. 11 tacet

3. Lis - ten to the wind, __ it won't lie to you. If you

Gtr. 8

mf
w/ slight dist.

Gtr. 2: w/ Rhy. Fig. 2 (2 1/2 times)

love it, let it go and watch it fly to you. __

Ev - 'ry set - ting sun __ gent - ly weeps. __

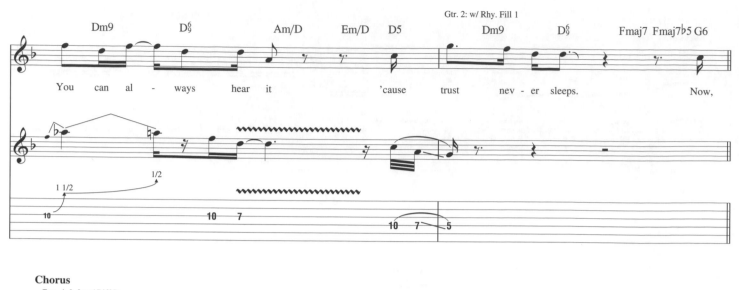

You can al - ways hear it 'cause trust nev - er sleeps. Now,

Chorus

they'll all want____ you to serve them, but the on - ly one you got to serve is your

Pitch: E

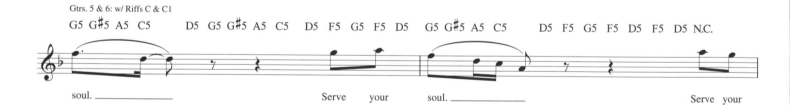

soul.____ Serve your soul.____ Serve your

soul.____ Serve your soul.___

Guitar Solo

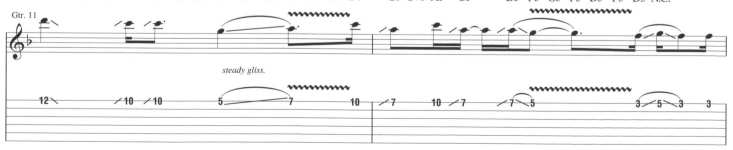

Interlude

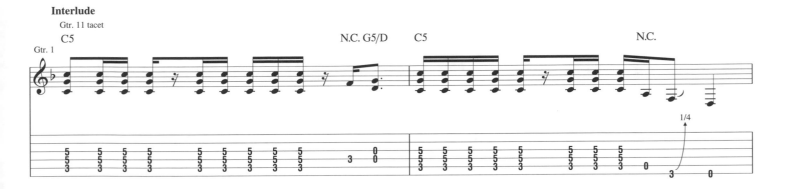

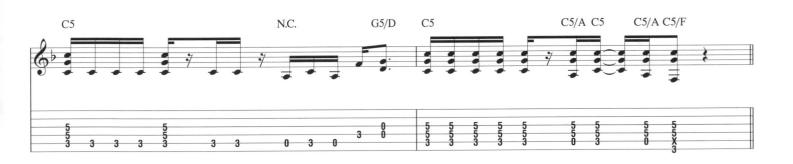

Outro

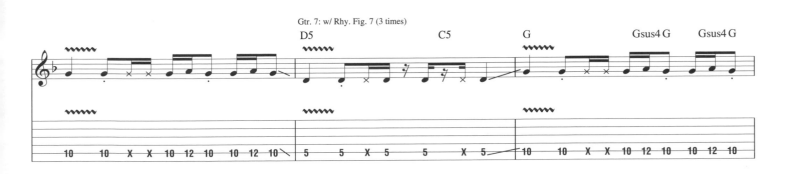

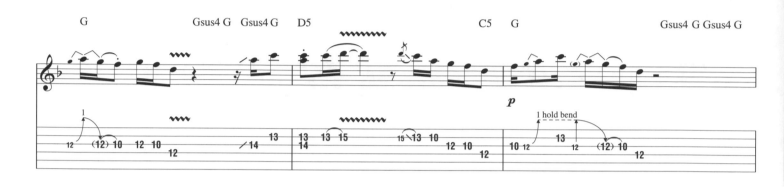

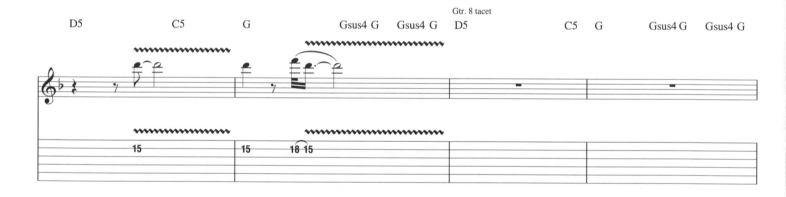

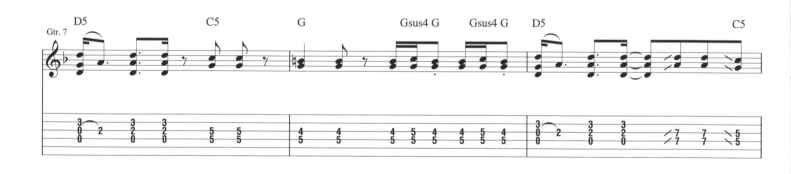

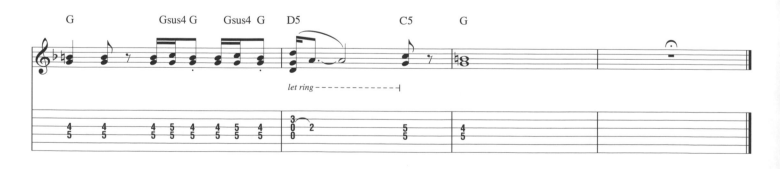

Guitar Notation Legend

Guitar Music can be notated three different ways: on a *musical staff*, in *tablature*, and in *rhythm slashes*.

RHYTHM SLASHES are written above the staff. Strum chords in the rhythm indicated. Use the chord diagrams found at the top of the first page of the transcription for the appropriate chord voicings. Round noteheads indicate single notes.

THE MUSICAL STAFF shows pitches and rhythms and is divided by bar lines into measures. Pitches are named after the first seven letters of the alphabet.

TABLATURE graphically represents the guitar fingerboard. Each horizontal line represents a a string, and each number represents a fret.

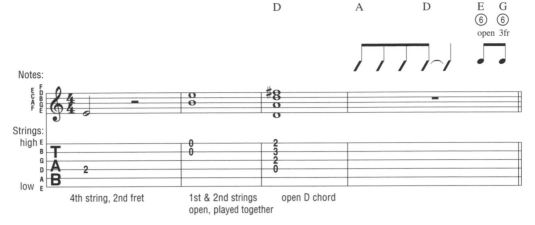

4th string, 2nd fret

1st & 2nd strings open, played together

open D chord

Definitions for Special Guitar Notation

HALF-STEP BEND: Strike the note and bend up 1/2 step.

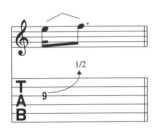

WHOLE-STEP BEND: Strike the note and bend up one step.

GRACE NOTE BEND: Strike the note and immediately bend up as indicated.

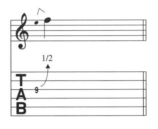

SLIGHT (MICROTONE) BEND: Strike the note and bend up 1/4 step.

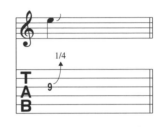

BEND AND RELEASE: Strike the note and bend up as indicated, then release back to the original note. Only the first note is struck.

PRE-BEND: Bend the note as indicated, then strike it.

PRE-BEND AND RELEASE: Bend the note as indicated. Strike it and release the bend back to the original note.

UNISON BEND: Strike the two notes simultaneously and bend the lower note up to the pitch of the higher.

VIBRATO: The string is vibrated by rapidly bending and releasing the note with the fretting hand.

WIDE VIBRATO: The pitch is varied to a greater degree by vibrating with the fretting hand.

HAMMER-ON: Strike the first (lower) note with one finger, then sound the higher note (on the same string) with another finger by fretting it without picking.

PULL-OFF: Place both fingers on the notes to be sounded. Strike the first note and without picking, pull the finger off to sound the second (lower) note.

LEGATO SLIDE: Strike the first note and then slide the same fret-hand finger up or down to the second note. The second note is not struck.

SHIFT SLIDE: Same as legato slide, except the second note is struck.

TRILL: Very rapidly alternate between the notes indicated by continuously hammering on and pulling off.

TAPPING: Hammer ("tap") the fret indicated with the pick-hand index or middle finger and pull off to the note fretted by the fret hand.

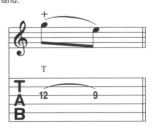

NATURAL HARMONIC: Strike the note while the fret-hand lightly touches the string directly over the fret indicated.

PINCH HARMONIC: The note is fretted normally and a harmonic is produced by adding the edge of the thumb or the tip of the index finger of the pick hand to the normal pick attack.

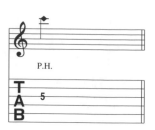

HARP HARMONIC: The note is fretted normally and a harmonic is produced by gently resting the pick hand's index finger directly above the indicated fret (in parentheses) while the pick hand's thumb or pick assists by plucking the appropriate string.

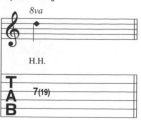

PICK SCRAPE: The edge of the pick is rubbed down (or up) the string, producing a scratchy sound.

MUFFLED STRINGS: A percussive sound is produced by laying the fret hand across the string(s) without depressing, and striking them with the pick hand.

PALM MUTING: The note is partially muted by the pick hand lightly touching the string(s) just before the bridge.

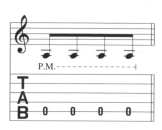

RAKE: Drag the pick across the strings indicated with a single motion.

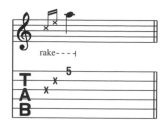

TREMOLO PICKING: The note is picked as rapidly and continuously as possible.

ARPEGGIATE: Play the notes of the chord indicated by quickly rolling them from bottom to top.

VIBRATO BAR DIVE AND RETURN: The pitch of the note or chord is dropped a specified number of steps (in rhythm) then returned to the original pitch.

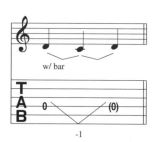

VIBRATO BAR SCOOP: Depress the bar just before striking the note, then quickly release the bar.

VIBRATO BAR DIP: Strike the note and then immediately drop a specified number of steps, then release back to the original pitch.

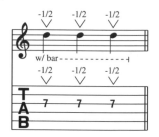

Additional Musical Definitions

> (accent)	• Accentuate note (play it louder)	
∧ (accent)	• Accentuate note with great intensity	
· (staccato)	• Play the note short	
⊓	• Downstroke	
∨	• Upstroke	

D.S. al Coda • Go back to the sign (𝄋), then play until the measure marked "**To Coda**," then skip to the section labelled "**Coda**."

D.C. al Fine • Go back to the beginning of the song and play until the measure marked "**Fine**" (end).

Rhy. Fig. • Label used to recall a recurring accompaniment pattern (usually chordal).

Riff • Label used to recall composed, melodic lines (usually single notes) which recur.

Fill • Label used to identify a brief melodic figure which is to be inserted into the arrangement.

Rhy. Fill • A chordal version of a Fill.

tacet • Instrument is silent (drops out).

 • Repeat measures between signs.

1. | 2. • When a repeated section has different endings, play the first ending only the first time and the second ending only the second time.

NOTE: Tablature numbers in parentheses mean:
1. The note is being sustained over a system (note in standard notation is tied), or
2. The note is sustained, but a new articulation (such as a hammer-on, pull-off, slide or vibrato begins), or
3. The note is a barely audible "ghost" note (note in standard notation is also in parentheses).